First World War
and Army of Occupation
War Diary
France, Belgium and Germany

29 DIVISION
88 Infantry Brigade
Essex Regiment
1st Battalion
27 January 1916 - 31 January 1918

WO95/2309/1

The Naval & Military Press Ltd
www.nmarchive.com
Published in association with The National Archives

Published by

The Naval & Military Press Ltd

Unit 10 Ridgewood Industrial Park,

Uckfield, East Sussex,

TN22 5QE England

Tel: +44 (0) 1825 749494

www.naval-military-press.com

www.nmarchive.com

This diary has been reprinted in facsimile from the original. Any imperfections are inevitably reproduced and the quality may fall short of modern type and cartographic standards.

© Crown Copyright
Images reproduced by permission of The National Archives, London, England, 2015.

Contents

Document type	Place/Title	Date From	Date To
Heading	WO95/2309/1		
Heading	29th Division 38th Infy Bde 1st Bn Essex Regt Mar 1916-1918 July To 37 Div. 112 Bde		
Heading	War Diary Appendix II		
Heading	29th Division. 88th Infantry Brigade. Arrived Marseilles from Egypt 20.3.16 1st Battalion Essex Regiment March 1916 Dec 1917		
War Diary	Shallufa East.	01/03/1916	01/03/1916
War Diary	Suez	02/03/1916	14/03/1916
War Diary	Alexandria.	15/03/1916	31/03/1916
Heading	29th Division. 88th Infantry Brigade. 1st Battalion Essex Regiment April 1916		
War Diary	Vauchelles Le-Domart	01/04/1916	01/04/1916
War Diary	Montrelet	02/04/1916	04/04/1916
War Diary	Louvencourt	04/04/1916	12/04/1916
War Diary	Englebelmer	12/04/1916	30/04/1916
Miscellaneous	From Lieut-General Sir Aylmer-Hunter-Weston, K.C.B., D.S.O.	25/04/1916	25/04/1916
Heading	29th Division. 88th Infantry Brigade. 1st Battalion Essex Regiment May 1916		
War Diary	Englebelmer	01/05/1916	08/05/1916
War Diary	Acheux	08/05/1916	18/05/1916
War Diary	Englebelmer	18/05/1916	28/05/1916
Heading	29th Division 88th Infantry Brigade. 1st Battalion Essex Regiment June 1916		
War Diary	Trenches	01/06/1916	07/06/1916
War Diary	Louvencourt	08/06/1916	14/06/1916
War Diary	Englebelmer	15/06/1916	22/06/1916
War Diary	Louvencourt	23/06/1916	30/06/1916
Miscellaneous	To the adjt 1/Essex Rgt		
Miscellaneous	Adjt C L T		
Miscellaneous	O.C. 1st Essex Regt.	16/06/1916	16/06/1916
Map			
Heading	29th Division 88th Infantry Brigade. 1st Battalion Essex Regiment July 1916		
War Diary	Trenches	01/07/1916	06/07/1916
War Diary	Mailly Wood	06/07/1916	10/07/1916
War Diary	Trenches.	10/07/1916	10/07/1916
War Diary	Acheux Wood	17/07/1916	23/07/1916
War Diary	Beauval	23/07/1916	27/07/1916
War Diary	Poperinghe	28/07/1916	30/07/1916
War Diary	Ypres.	31/07/1916	31/07/1916
Miscellaneous	(Duplicate). Messages And Signals.		
Miscellaneous	C Form (Duplicate). Messages And Signals.		
Miscellaneous	A Form. Messages And Signals.		
Miscellaneous	C Form (Duplicate). Messages And Signals.		
Miscellaneous	A Form. Messages And Signals.		
Miscellaneous	C Form (Duplicate). Messages And Signals.		
Miscellaneous	C Form (Original). Messages And Signals.		
Miscellaneous	A Form. Messages And Signals.		

Heading	29th Division 88th Infantry Brigade. 1st Battalion Essex Regiment August 1916		
Heading	War Diary of 1st Bn the Essex Regiment. from August 1st to August 31st-1916		
War Diary	Ypres.	01/08/1916	08/08/1916
War Diary	Firing Line	09/08/1916	19/08/1916
War Diary	'O' Camp	20/08/1916	29/08/1916
War Diary	Firing Line	30/08/1916	31/08/1916
Heading	29th Division. 88th Infantry Brigade. 1st Battalion Essex Regiment September 1916		
Heading	War Diary of 1st Bn. the Essex Regt. from 1-9-16 to 30-9-16 (Volume)		
War Diary	Trenches.	01/09/1916	08/09/1916
War Diary	Ypres.	09/09/1916	18/09/1916
War Diary	'O' Camp	19/09/1916	27/09/1916
War Diary	Ypres	29/09/1916	30/09/1916
Heading	29th Division. 88th Infantry Brigade. 1st Battalion Essex Regiment October 1916		
Heading	War Diary of 1st Bn. the Essex Regiment from 1st October 1916 to 31st October 1916 (Volume)		
War Diary	Ypres.	01/10/1916	04/10/1916
War Diary	Poperinghe	04/10/1916	07/10/1916
War Diary	Corbie	08/10/1916	09/10/1916
War Diary	Trenches	10/10/1916	20/10/1916
War Diary	Bernafay Camp	21/10/1916	26/10/1916
War Diary	Trenches	26/10/1916	28/10/1916
War Diary	Bernafay Camp	29/10/1916	30/10/1916
War Diary	Mericourt L'Abbe	31/10/1916	31/10/1916
Operation(al) Order(s)	O.O. No. 18 10/11/16 1/Essex October 1916	10/11/1916	10/11/1916
Operation(al) Order(s)	Operation Order No 19 by Lt Col A.C Halahan Comdg 1st Essex Regt	11/10/1916	11/10/1916
Miscellaneous	Operation Orders By Lt Col. A.C Halahan.	17/10/1916	17/10/1916
Operation(al) Order(s)	Addenda To Operation Order No. 20		
Heading	29th Division. 88th Infantry Brigade. 1st Battalion Essex Regiment November 1916		
Heading	War Diary of 1st Bn. The Essex Regiment (Volume 20) From 1.11 16 to 30.11.16		
War Diary	Mericourt L'Abbe	01/11/1916	15/11/1916
War Diary	Meaulte	15/11/1916	17/11/1916
War Diary	Trones Wood	17/11/1916	21/11/1916
War Diary	Firing Line	21/11/1916	24/11/1916
War Diary	N Carnoy	24/11/1916	30/11/1916
Heading	29th Division. 88th Infantry Brigade. 1st Battalion Essex Regiment December 1916		
Heading	War Diary of 1st Battalion The Essex Regiment. From 1st December. 1916 to 31st December 1916 (Volume) 20		
War Diary	Firing Line	01/12/1916	02/12/1916
War Diary	Bernafay	03/12/1916	03/12/1916
War Diary	Carnoy	04/12/1916	07/12/1916
War Diary	Bernafay	07/12/1916	07/12/1916
War Diary	Firing Line	08/12/1916	11/12/1916
War Diary	Carnoy	12/12/1916	12/12/1916
War Diary	Ville	12/12/1916	13/12/1916
War Diary	Conde	14/12/1916	14/12/1916
War Diary	Montagne	15/12/1916	31/12/1916

Heading	War Diary 1st Battalion Essex Regt. From 1st January 1917 to 31st January 1917 By Essex Regt. Volumne 23		
War Diary	Montagne	01/01/1917	11/01/1917
War Diary	Corbie	12/01/1917	15/01/1917
War Diary	Meaulte	15/01/1917	16/01/1917
War Diary	Carnoy	17/01/1917	17/01/1917
War Diary	Guillemont	18/01/1917	18/01/1917
War Diary	Firing Line	19/01/1917	20/01/1917
War Diary	Guillemont	23/01/1917	23/01/1917
War Diary	Firing Line	25/01/1917	26/01/1917
War Diary	Guillemont Carnoy	27/01/1916	27/01/1916
War Diary	Guillemont	28/01/1916	31/01/1916
Heading	War Diary of 1st Bn The Essex Regiment for February 1917 (Volume 23.) G. West. 15. N.		
War Diary	Carnoy	01/02/1917	02/02/1917
War Diary	Guillemont	03/02/1917	04/02/1917
War Diary	Firing Line	04/02/1917	07/02/1917
War Diary	Carnoy	07/02/1917	08/02/1917
War Diary	Cardonette	09/02/1917	18/02/1917
War Diary	Fregicourt	21/02/1917	22/02/1917
War Diary	Firing Line	22/02/1917	23/02/1917
War Diary	Fregicourt	24/02/1917	25/02/1917
War Diary	Bronfay	25/02/1917	27/02/1917
War Diary	Combles	27/02/1917	28/02/1917
Heading	War Diary of 1st Bn. The Essex Regt. For. March 1917. (Volume 25)		
War Diary	Firing Line.	01/03/1917	01/03/1917
War Diary	Fregicourt.	02/03/1917	02/03/1917
War Diary	Bronfay	03/03/1917	04/03/1917
War Diary	Meaulte	05/03/1917	20/03/1917
War Diary	Montagne	20/03/1917	28/03/1917
War Diary	Picquigny	29/03/1917	29/03/1917
War Diary	Flesselles	30/03/1917	31/03/1917
Heading	War Diary of 1st Bn The Essex Regt for April 1917 (Volume 26)		
War Diary	Flesselles	01/04/1917	02/04/1917
War Diary	Mondicourt	03/04/1917	05/04/1917
War Diary	Ivergny	06/04/1917	07/04/1917
War Diary	Humbercourt	08/04/1917	12/04/1917
War Diary	Line.	13/04/1917	14/04/1917
War Diary	Arras	15/04/1917	30/04/1917
Heading	(Temporary) War Diary of 1st Bn. The Essex Regt for April 1917 (Volume 26.)		
War Diary	Flesselles	01/04/1917	30/04/1917
Heading	War Diary of 1st Bn. The Essex Regt. for May 1917. (Volume 27)		
War Diary	Boyencourt	01/05/1917	02/05/1917
War Diary	Arras.	03/05/1917	31/05/1917
Heading	War Diary 1st Essex Regt From of June 1917 To 30th June 1916 (Volume No 28)		
War Diary	Arras.	01/06/1917	05/06/1917
War Diary	Montrelet	06/06/1917	27/06/1917
War Diary	Proven	28/06/1917	30/06/1917
Heading	War Diary of 1st Bn The Essex Regiment for Month of July 1917. (Volume 29)		
War Diary	E. of Proven	01/07/1917	04/07/1917

War Diary	S.E. of Eykhoek	05/07/1917	05/07/1917
War Diary	L.2. Defences	06/07/1917	09/07/1917
War Diary	In The Line	10/07/1917	10/07/1917
War Diary	S.E. of Crombeke	12/07/1917	19/07/1917
War Diary	S. Of Haringhe	20/07/1917	23/07/1917
War Diary	S.E. Of Crombeke	24/07/1917	24/07/1917
War Diary	De Whippe Cabaret	25/07/1917	28/07/1917
War Diary	S.E Of Crombeke	29/07/1917	31/07/1917
Heading	War Diary of 1st Bn. The Essex Regt for August 1917. (Volume 30).		
War Diary		01/08/1917	31/08/1917
Heading	War Diary of 1st Bn. Essex. Regiment From 1st September 1917 To 30th September 191 Volume No 31		
War Diary	Putney Camp	01/09/1917	11/09/1917
War Diary	Herzeele	12/09/1917	16/09/1917
War Diary	Putney Camp.	17/09/1917	20/09/1917
War Diary	Dulwich Camp	21/09/1917	21/09/1917
War Diary	In The Line	22/09/1917	25/09/1917
War Diary	Dulwich Camp	26/09/1917	28/09/1917
War Diary	H. Camp	29/09/1917	30/09/1917
Heading	War Diary of 1st Bn. Essex Regiment From 1st October 1917 To 31st October 1917 (Volume No. 32)		
War Diary		01/10/1917	31/10/1917
Heading	War Diary of 1st Bn. Essex Regiment From 1st Bn. Essex Regiment From 1st November, 1917 To 30th November, 1917 (Volume No. 33)		
Heading	War Diary of 1st Bn. The Essex Regt For November 1917 (Vol. 33)		
War Diary	Pommier.	01/11/1917	30/11/1917
Heading	War Diary of 1st Bn. Essex Regt From 1st Decr 1917 To 31st Decr 1917 (Volume No. 34)		
War Diary		01/12/1917	19/12/1917
Miscellaneous	Herewith War Diary of 1st Batt Essex Regt. For Month of January. 1918	13/03/1918	13/03/1918
Miscellaneous	War Diary Of 1st Bn The Essex Regiment For Month Of January 1918. Volume 35		
War Diary	Royan (Lebiez)	01/01/1918	31/01/1918

MO95/2309

29TH DIVISION
88TH INFY BDE

1ST BN ESSEX REGT
MAR 1916 - DEC 1917
1918 inx

To
37 DIV.
112 Bde

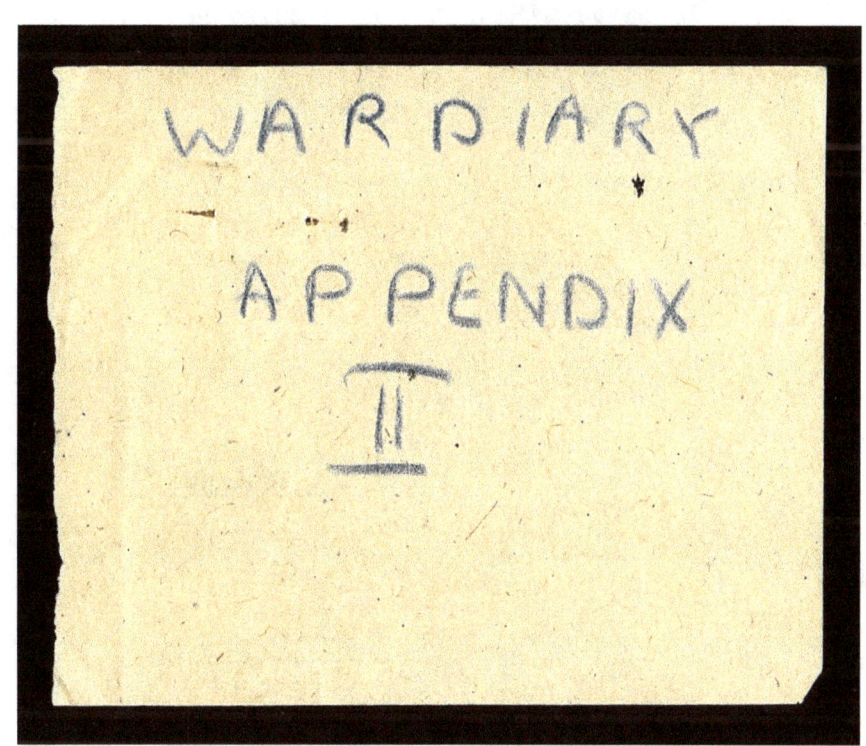

29th Division.
88th Infantry Brigade.

Arrived MARSEILLES from EGYPT 20.3.16.

1st BATTALION

ESSEX REGIMENT

MARCH 1916

Dec 1917

Army Form C. 2118.

WAR DIARY
INTELLIGENCE SUMMARY.
(Erase heading not required.)

Instructions regarding War Diaries and Intelligence Summaries are contained in F.S. Regs., Part II and the Staff Manual respectively. Title pages will be prepared in manuscript.

Place	Date	Hour	Summary of Events and Information	Remarks and references to Appendices.
SHALLUFA EAST.	1-3-16	6.p.m	"W" and "X" Coys rejoined the Battalion from ARDWICK-POST.	
SUEZ	2-3-16	6.p.m	Battalion returned to SUEZ by Route March.	
	2nd/6/13th-3-16	6.p.m	Remained at SUEZ. Lieut. Col. H.T.T. Rice left the Battalion for England. Capt. J.J. Noyse took over Command.	
SUEZ.	14-3-16	6.p.m	Entrained at SUEZ in two parties and arrived at ALEXANDRIA the following morning	
ALEXANDRIA.	15-3-16	6.p.m	Embarked at ALEXANDRIA on H.T. TRANSYLVANIA, strength 33 Officers 1002 other ranks, sailed at 7.15 p.m.	
	15th/16/19	6.p.m	At Sea.	
	20-3-16	6.p.m	Arrived MARSEILLES - 7am - Disembarked 10.30 pm and entrained at 1am.	
	21-3-16	6.p.m	In the train	
	22-3-16	6.p.m	do	
	23-3-16	6.p.m	Arrived PONT REMY 4.20 a.m. Proceeded by march route to billets in BELLANCOURT.	
	23rd/30	6 p.m	At BELLANCOURT.	
	31-3-16	6.p.m	Proceeded by march route to VAUCHELLES - L - DOMART and went into billets there.	

J.C.Owen Captain
Adjutant 1st Bn Essex Regt
17.4.16

29th Division.

88th Infantry Brigade.

1st BATTALION

ESSEX REGIMENT

APRIL 1 9 1 6

Army Form C. 2118.

WAR DIARY
or
INTELLIGENCE SUMMARY.
(Erase heading not required.)

April 1916   1st Mon. Regt.

Place	Date	Hour	Summary of Events and Information	Remarks and references to Appendices
VAUC HELLES & MONT DONART	1.4.16	9am	Proceeded by route march to MONTRELET arriving 1.45pm Strength 29 Officers 1000 Other ranks	
MONTRELET 2-4			at Billets Captain F.C. DINAN & Lieut H.R. BAINES joined Bn on 2.4.16	
LOUVENCOURT	4-12	9.45	Proceeded by route march to LOUVENCOURT arriving 5pm at billets	
	12	5pm	Marched to ENGLEBELMER arriving 8.30pm	
ENGLEBELMER	12-30		at Billets, Brigade reserve. Garrisoned FORTS — MOULIN, + PROWSE, B. employed in [illeg] day in making trenches, POMPADOUR St, started by 2nd Bn, finished, Major A. CLUTTERBUCK & Capt J.J. MOYSE wounded	
	15		J.R. MEIKLEJOHN, 1st Border Regt joined Bn to assume Command	
	16		General Sir AYLMER, HUNTER-WESTON on anniversary of landing on GALLIPOLI inspected those who took part in the landing, & congratulated them, 1190 men & 2 Officers	
	25		General de L'ISLE congratulated Bn on work done on Trenches	
	20		Copy of Message from General Hunter-Weston attached.	

FROM   Lieut-General Sir Aylmer Hunter-Weston, K.C.B., D.S.O.

TO   All Officers and Men of the incomparable 29th Division,
       who took part with him in the historic landing on the
       Gallipoli Peninsula, 25th April, 1915.

On this, the first anniversary of the landing effected by the incomparable 29th Division near Cape Helles on the Gallipoli Peninsula, I send to each officer and man, who took part in that glorious operation of war, my personal greetings and congratulations on the privilege and opportunity which was accorded to you of being able to do so much for our beloved King and Country.

As fore-shadowed in the personal note I sent to each of you before we landed, you had to face death by bullet, by shell, by mine, by drowning. But nothing deterred either you that are here with me now, or those even more glorious comrades that have gone across the Great Divide and have attained the most noble end that can befall any man. It was your discipline, your training, and your fine esprit-de-corps that enabled you to carry on, notwithstanding your heavy losses, to stick it out, and to win through. You were successful in all the many engagements we fought together on the South end of the Peninsula, and the fact that our troops subsequently evacuated the Peninsula in no way dims the glory of your achievements. Indeed, the success of both the evacuations were greatly due to your good work.

In the great operations, which must come before this war is won by us, and in which we hope that it may be our good fortune to bear a leading part, I know that the 29th Division may always be relied on to emulate the noble example that it set itself a year ago today. This can only be if the officers and men, who have joined the Division in the past 12 months, determine that their discipline and spirit shall be of as high an order as that that enabled their predecessors to gain so glorious a place on the Roll of Fame.

I consider myself highly honoured to have the 29th Division under my command, and I look forward to taking part with it again in many a victorious fight.

AYLMER HUNTER-WESTON.
Lt-GENERAL.

Headquarters,
VIII Army Corps.
25th April, 1916.

29th Division.

88th Infantry Brigade

1st BATTALION

ESSEX REGIMENT

MAY 1916

Army Form C. 2118.

WAR DIARY
or
INTELLIGENCE SUMMARY.
(Erase heading not required.)

1st Bn. the Essex Regt. Page 9
1 – 31st May 1916.

Place	Date	Hour	Summary of Events and Information	Remarks and references to Appendices
ENGLEBELMER	1st & 3rd May	8 pm	Relieve Borders Regt in the trenches, right & left sector. 2 Coys in firing line, 1 Coy in support & 1 Coy in reserve in AUCHONVILLERS.	
	3 & 8		In the trenches. Very little rifle or shell fire - only 2 casualties, 2nd Lieut. A. Croucher Jones Bn.	
ACHEUX	8th	10.30 pm	Relieved by Royal Dublin Fusiliers & march into billets at ACHEUX.	
	8 – 15		Bn employed in finding Working Parties. Captain Naseton rejoined. The following Officers Joined Bn. Lieut. A.T. Renton, 2nd Lieuts. F.R. Wheatley, C.P. Leonard, G.A. Apps, T.M.F. Whitby, J.T. Broomfield, M.L.W. Kotright.	
			2nd Bn. K. hot Refts AC BERTRANCOURT 2 miles from	
	18th	7.30 pm	March to ENGLEBELMER. Strength 1030 all ranks.	
ENGLEBELMER	18 – 28		Divisional Reserve, digging trenches.	
	20th		Major A.C. Holahan Joined Bn & took over command.	
	24th		Major Tempry Lt. Col. T. Lenward – Kelly DSO. to Hospital Joined Bn & took over command.	
	28th	2.30	Relieve Royal Fusiliers in the trenches, disposition as before.	

(signed) *Whitehurst*
Lieut. Colonel
Commanding 1st Bn. Essex Regiment

29th Division
88th Infantry Brigade

1st BATTALION

ESSEX REGIMENT

JUNE 1916

WAR DIARY
INTELLIGENCE SUMMARY

1st Battn. ESSEX Regiment

Army Form C. 2118.

Place	Date	Hour	Summary of Events and Information	Remarks and references to Appendices
TRENCHES	1.6.16 to 7.6.16		Firing line left sector of divisional line, in front of AUCHONVILLERS. Lt. Colonel J. SHERWOOD-KELLY D.S.O. wounded 4.6.16. Lt. Colonel A.C. HALAHAN took over command. 2nd Lt. JACKSON joined & Lt. McKean rejoined as an officer. Lt. CAROLIN & 2nd Lt. PURKISS-GINN joined, & 2nd Lt. READ and 2nd Lt. CHESHIRE rejoined on 4.6. On inspection of 3/4th LANCASHIRE FUS. made a raid thro' our lines.	
LOUVENCOURT	8.6.16 to 14.6.16		Went back into divisional reserve at Louvencourt. An inspection of 7/R. and after several days practising an attack, the Brigade went up into Brigade reserve for next sector of the divisional line at ENGLEBELMER. Brigade working parties chiefly R.E. took up nearly the whole Battn. Remainder improved the trenches from which we were ultimately to attack.	
ENGLEBELMER	15.6.16 to 22.6.16			
LOUVENCOURT	23.6.16		Returned to Louvencourt. Lt. BARTLEET & 4 men wounded in trenches on 25th. Capt. MOORE evacuated sick on 27th. Capt. GRUNE rejoined 1st Battn. on 29th.	
	24.6.16 to 30.6.16		Bombardment of German trenches commenced and continued increasingly day & night together with discharges of smoke & gas. 29/30th 0 park of 7 30 men and Lt. RUSSELL, Lt. WARNER & 2nd Lt. MORISON raided the German trenches, opposite MARY REDAN. The first wire listening patrol, killed one German and pulled a dug out. The whole party got back to "B" Coy. trenches, after remaining in German trench for 20 minutes.	

Army Form C. 2118.

WAR DIARY
or
INTELLIGENCE SUMMARY.
(Erase heading not required.)

Place	Date	Hour	Summary of Events and Information	Remarks and references to Appendices
LOUVENCOURT	25th		Bde. practising for attack on German trenches. Objectives allotted to Division as follows:- German Trenches Ref:- (a) Q17B35.4 to Q5C2.8 including village of BEAUMONT-HAMEL. (b) 2nd line R7C9.4 to ...41. Q6D4.0 including BEAUCOURT. (c) 3rd line R8B8.2 and .0.9. to point R2134.0. (a)+(b) allotted to 86th & 87th Bdes. (c) to 88 th Bde. The 4th Div. attacking simultaneously on its left & 36th on its right. Attack practised in 4 stages. 1st Advance from own trenches to STATION ROAD 2nd From STATION RD to ARTILLERY LANE 3rd From ARTILLERY LANE to PUISIEUX RD 4th From PUISIEUX RD to GERMAN 3rd line trenches. Objective allotted to ESSEX Regt. from R8B0.4 to R2D9.3. The N.F.L.D. Regt. being on its left and 1st HAMPSHIRE Regt. & WORCESTER Regt. in support. Formation of Attack. Coys. in platoon columns, distances between sections 25 yds. " " " platoons 40 " " " Coys. 100 "	

Army Form C. 2118.

WAR DIARY
or
INTELLIGENCE SUMMARY.
(Erase heading not required.)

Place	Date	Hour	Summary of Events and Information	Remarks and references to Appendices
LOUVENCOURT	25th		Advance to be in front of this coy. Y on the right, X on the left, with W & Z coys. in support and one section, 88th M.G.S. attached, Z coy. then f. the smoke duty coy. After clearing the bend of the river at R8 B1. 4. half of troops to protect Y's right & the river.	
	28th 16 30th		Orders received postponing the date of attack. British lent 10% deft. back on reinforcements, left howeve until 9 p.m. Strong they officers before the attack. brot in 5 front, strength of other ranks was 840.	

To the Adjt
1/Essex Rgt.

Lieut Eastwood has gone up
to KNIGHTSBRIDGE to check
quantity & condition of Stores.
These will be removed to
Divisional Dumps to-night
& in trucks on the light railway
behind ST JOHNS ROAD.

SH M Paxton Capt
O.C. Z Coy

Handed in at C+Q	Office 0050	Received	m.

TO AA1/64T

Sender's Number	Day of Month	In reply to Number	AAA
25 1000	14		

Can the Ration Dump at Sandpit be handed in by DAJ AAA 47 do please do and report quantity and condition to this office

FROM C+Q

PLACE & TIME

A.2.7
14.7.16

C.R.Mr. Peter

Secret

Please return

O. C.

    1st Essex Regt.

        Reference to Operation Order No. 36, dated 14th June sent you yesterday; please find attached copy of Trench Diagram.

                                                Staff Captain,

16th June, 1916.   Brigade Major, 88th Brigade.

29th Division.
88th Infantry Brigade

1st BATTALION

ESSEX REGIMENT

J U L Y 1 9 1 6

WAR DIARY or INTELLIGENCE SUMMARY.

Army Form C. 2118.

Place	Date	Hour	Summary of Events and Information	Remarks and references to Appendices
TRENCHES	1.7.16		List of Officers who took part in the attack on July 1st 1916.	
			Lt. Col. A.C. HALAHAN. Lieut. F.F. COOKE (W) Lieut. A.P. CHAWNER.	
			Capt. F.C. DINAN 2Lieut. W.R. CHESHIRE (K) " C.R. LAWSON.	
			Capt. A.D. HENDERSON (W) " R.B. HORWOOD (K) " G.A. APPS.	
			Capt. A.M. PAXTON " E.T.H. HILL (W) " M.C.W. WORTRIGHT.	
			Capt. T.A.C. BRABAZON (W) " H.A. JACKSON (W) " A. GRANT.	
			Capt. A.N.W. POWELL " A.J. MORISON (W) " B. HULL.	
			Lieut. H.A. HARVEY " B.O. WARNER (W) " F.R. WHEATLEY	
			Lieut. R.E.C. CAROLIN " W.J. McLEAN " J.T. BROOMFIELD.	
			M.O. Capt. F. SAUNDERS 2Lt. A. COUCHER (BATTLE POLICE.) Other ranks "roughly" 840.	
	1.7.16	3.30am	Took up position in ST. JOHN'S ROAD (ref Trench Map) as follows:- W Coy's right in FRENCH TRENCH Z, Y, + X Coys left being on UXBRIDGE ROAD. Men much fatigued by long time (9hr. 30m - 3.30am 1st) it had taken to get into position and heavy equipment carried.	
		6.0am	Intense artillery bombardment commenced.	
		7.20am	Mine exploded under HAWTHORNE REDOUBT.	
		7.30am	86th & 87th Brigades left our 1st Line trenches, to assault their objective. Heavy Artillery	

Army Form C.-2118.

WAR DIARY
or
INTELLIGENCE SUMMARY.
(Erase heading not required.)

Instructions regarding War Diaries and Intelligence Summaries are contained in F. S. Regs., Part II. and the Staff Manual respectively. Title pages will be prepared in manuscript.

Place	Date	Hour	Summary of Events and Information	Remarks and references to Appendices
TRENCHES.	1-7-16	7.30am	and Machine Gun fire, and difficulty of getting through our own wire caused these other very heavy losses. Very few men survived long enough to enable them to reach half way across "No Man's Land".	
		8.40am →	Orders received cancelling our previous objective and ordering ESSEX and NFLD. to advance and clear up German & their trenches. WNCLD. and Hants. remaining in reserve. N.F.L.D. were ordered to advance to the attack from their positions in ST. JOHN'S ROAD. ESSEX owing to ground between ST. JOHN'S ROAD and our front line being under heavy fire, were ordered to advance via communication trenches and take up a position on our front line from which to commence the assault. ESSEX and NFLD. Regt. to advance to the assault independently as soon as they were ready.	
		8.45am	Orders issued to Coys. to take up the following formations:— Very with its right in front 100 yds. N. of MARY REDAN. X Coy. to prolong to the left. W & Z Coys. being in support. NFLD. on the left were seen to advance from ST. JOHN'S ROAD and immediately came under very heavy arty. rifle	

WAR DIARY
INTELLIGENCE SUMMARY
(Erase heading not required.)

Army Form C. 2118.

Place	Date	Hour	Summary of Events and Information	Remarks and references to Appendices
TRENCHES			Prussians which practically wiped them out before 11Bg had gone many yards beyond our front line.	
		10.30am	Y coy. reported that 11Bg were in position in trenches with W Coy. Z coy. had taken up a position between X & Y coys. owing to the evaporation of the trenches due to being checked with accumulated and badly damaged by shell fire, it had taken Coy. two hours to get into position. Orders issued to Coys. to attack. Coys. came under Heavy A.R. M.Gun barrage immediately this advance over the parapet, causing heavy losses. Reports received from O.C. X coy. that our wire in two places had not been cut, that for 150 yards on each side of this gap he had suffered heavy casualties. Z coy. in Centre was able to make little progress. One platoon under Lt. CHAWNER getting about halfway across "NO MANS LAND." W coy. attempted to support, X were unable to make much progress.	
		11.10am	Lt SMITH. R.F.A. attached, learned from his front, that about an advance of the 1st German line was ordered from 11.10am to 12.30pm. Orders were immediately given because the attack and reorganize	

Army Form C. 2118.

WAR DIARY
INTELLIGENCE SUMMARY.
(Erase heading not required.)

Instructions regarding War Diaries and Intelligence Summaries are contained in F.S. Regs., Part II. and the Staff Manual respectively. Title pages will be prepared in manuscript.

Place	Date	Hour	Summary of Events and Information	Remarks and references to Appendices
TRENCHES.		11.10am	and surprise in ST. JOHNS ROAD, but it was only from the 2 Coys. the message to 2 Coy.	
		11.30am	Communication established with Bde. and orders received to renew the attack at 12.30pm.	
		11.55am	Orders issued to Coys. to prepare for the renewal of attack at 12.30pm.	
		12.20pm	Message received from Bde. postponing the attack to 12.45 pm. Brigade informed that owing to casualties and disorganisation, it was impossible to renew the attack until we had had time to reorganise. Subsequent orders received, cancelling the attack and ordering us to hold the line MARY REDAN – NEW TRENCH – REGENT STREET, getting in touch with the Worc. on our left and the 36 I.D. on the right and be prepared to repel counter attack. B's occupying above position with one coy. in support in ST. JOHNS ROAD.	
		3.30pm	Orders received that 7/15 Worc. were to relieve us in the firing line. Coys. on relief were to go into ST. JOHNS ROAD.	
		10.30pm	Head of Worc. arrived at KNIGHTSBRIDGE and Coys. notified and ordered 15 Road.	

WAR DIARY or INTELLIGENCE SUMMARY

(Erase heading not required.)

Army Form C. 2118.

Instructions regarding War Diaries and Intelligence Summaries are contained in F.S. Regs., Part II. and the Staff Manual respectively. Title pages will be prepared in manuscript.

Place	Date	Hour	Summary of Events and Information	Remarks and references to Appendices
TRENCHES		11.4pm	Relief cancelled and orders received to resume lost trenches.	
	July 2nd	3 am	Ordered to take up position in FETTHARD STREET, night on UXBRIDGE ROAD, left on LIMERICK JUNCTION. The line was found to be that of MONMOUTH REGT; orders received to take up position in ST JOHN'S ROAD left on THURLES DUMP, right on PICCADILLY.	
	July 3rd	5 am	Went into reserve, then into support to Hants, in St Johns Road.	
	4th	6 pm	Lt. Col. V.L. Powis rejoined from course at Flixecourt.	
MAILLY WOOD	8th to 9th		Moved to Mailly Wood. Two drafts, 70 Northamptons, and 20 Essex Regt, joined. General Hunter-Weston inspected the Battalion. Lifting night and day in the Commemorative Trenches, Bath Strength 611. (Beaudroft)	
TRENCHES	10/16		Moved up into firing line and relieved Hants. line extended from trench ROAD to P. Street, it was afterwards prolonged to D. Street. Heavy shelling most of the time; casualties were fairly heavy. Lt. Russell was killed. Boys in firing line and we in left of.	
ACHEUX WOOD	17 1/2 to 23rd		Moved to Acheux Wood, and received a course for dressing Baths, training at Hornecourt on Lewis only.	

1577 Wt. W10791/1773 500,000 1/15 D.D.&L. A.D.S.S./Forms/C. 2118.

WAR DIARY
INTELLIGENCE SUMMARY.
(Erase heading not required.)

Army Form C. 2118.

Instructions regarding War Diaries and Intelligence Summaries are contained in F. S. Regs., Part II. and the Staff Manual respectively. Title pages will be prepared in manuscript.

Place	Date	Hour	Summary of Events and Information	Remarks and references to Appendices
	23rd	9 a.m.	Moved to Beauval. Brigade made use of from 9 a.m. till 3 p.m. Went into billets, arranged by billeting party which went ahead early in the morning.	
BEAUVAL	23rd to 26th		Remained at Beauval. 25th Brigade returned to the Army. The remainder of the day parades were under company arrangements.	
	27th		Battalion entrained at Candas and reached HOOPOITRE Station at 3 a.m.	
POPERINGHE	27/28 28/7/15 29/7 to 30/7		on 28th. Batt. marched to POPERINGHE and went into billets. Battalion remained at Poperinghe. On night of 30th battalion moved to YPRES and went into billets in the town.	
YPRES	31st		Billeted in YPRES.	

Wakelow Lt. Colonel.
Comdg. 1st Bn. The Essex Regt.
31.7.16.

(Duplicate). Army Form C. 2123.
MESSAGES AND SIGNALS.   No. of Message

SM FORM 17	Charges to Pay. £ s. d.	Office Stamp.
AZQ Lt6 Goodey g		AZT 1-7-16

Service Instructions. AZQ

Handed in at .... Office .... m. Received .... m.

TO   ALL BATTALIONS

Sender's Number	Day of Month	In reply to Number	AAA
BM1810	1st		

Please report without delay estimated casualties in officers and other ranks

Also require exact map square of Essex Hd Qrs.

FROM
PLACE & TIME   AZQ

Phone J Goodey Lt

"C" Form (Duplicate). Army Form C. 2123.
MESSAGES AND SIGNALS. No. of Message ....

| | Charges to Pay. | Office Stamp. |
| | £   s.   d. | |

Service Instructions.

Handed in at A.2.A .... Office .... m. Received .... m.

TO ESSEX REGT

| Sender's Number | Day of Month | In reply to Number | AAA |
| BM9940 | 1st | | |

Reported that you have not yet taken over right of firing line from Inniskillings AAA will you please look into it and if you have not done so please do so and see that you are in touch with 36th Division on your right

FROM
PLACE & TIME   A.2.A

"A" Form.
MESSAGES AND SIGNALS.
Army Form C. 2121

Prefix	Code	m.	Words	Charge		This message is on a/c of:		Recd. at	m.
Office of Origin and Service Instructions.								No. of Message	
			Sent						
AZQ			At	m.		Service.		Date	
			To					From	
			By		(Signature of "Franking Officer.")			By	

TO — Worcestershire Regt & Essex Regt

Sender's Number	Day of Month	In reply to Number	
BM 1740	1.		AAA

Worcestershire Regt will take ground to their right. Junction between Worcestershire & Essex will be Junction of Regent St & Firing Line. AAA Firing line will be held as usual by posts with remainder of men for in support line.

R.R. Wilson
J.R. Mitton Cpt

From ....
Place ....

forwarded as now corrected. (Z)
Censor. Signature of Addressor or person authorised to telegraph in his name.
* This line should be erased if not required.

"A" Form.
MESSAGES AND SIGNALS.
Army Form C. 2121

Code	Words	Charge	This message is on a/c of:	Recd. at	m.
Office of Origin and Service Instructions.	Sent			Date	
	At	m.	Service.	From	
	To			By	
	By		(Signature of "Franking Officer.")		

TO: All Batts.
Major Spencer Smith
88th Machine Gun Coy.

Sender's Number: B.M. 14.25
Day of Month: 1
AAA

Worcestershire Regiment will remain in their present position in the firing line aaa Essex Regiment will hold the remainder firing line and support trenches. aaa The right of Worcestershire Regiment to junction with 36th Division aaa The Hampshire Regiment will hold Fethard Street from Carlisle Street. aaa The Newfoundland Regiment will hold the support trenches from St James Street to the right. aaa 10% reinforcements will rejoin their Batts. aaa These dispositions are for the purpose of repelling a counter attack should one be made aaa The Worcestershire and Hampshire Regiments will be prepared to attack (if ordered) in depth. Each Batt in two lines Worcestershire Regt leading

From
Place
Time

The above may be forwarded as now corrected. (Z)
Censor. Signature of Addressor or person authorised to telegraph in his name.
* This line should be erased if not required.

"A" Form.
MESSAGES AND SIGNALS.
Army Form C. 2121
No. of Message _____

Code ___ m.	Words	Charge	This message is on a/c of:	Recd. at ___ m.
nd Service Instructions.	Sent			Date
	At ___ m.		_____ Service.	From
	To			
	By		(Signature of "Franking Officer.")	By

TO

Sender's Number	Day of Month	In reply to Number	
* BM 1425	1		**AAA**

and Hampshire Regiment in support aaa
The 88th Machine Gun Coy will take up a
position to cover the front against
possible counter attack. aaa

Altenhuun Clarken Maj
for Bde Major

From: 88th Bde
Place:
Time:

The above may be forwarded as now corrected.   (Z)

Censor.   Signature of Addressor or person authorised to telegraph in his name.

* This line should be erased if not required.

"C" For... (Duplicate). Army Form C. 2123.
MESSAGES AND SIGNALS. No. of Message............

| Service Instructions. | SM AZQ S/C Gooday | Charges to Pay. £ s. d. | Office Stamp. AZ? 1-7-1. |

Handed in at............... Office......... m. Received......... m.

TO ALL BATTALIONS

| Sender's Number | Day of Month | In reply to Number | AAA |
| BM1505 | | | |

Please return any men of 87th Bde in your trenches back to St Johns Rd to reorganise

FROM
PLACE & TIME AZQ

Phone J Gooday L/C

"A" Form. Army Form C. 2121.
MESSAGES AND SIGNALS.

Prefix	Code	m.	Words	Charge	This message is on a/c of:		Recd. at	m.
Office of Origin and Service Instructions.			Sent				Date	
			At	m.		Service.	From	
			To				By	
			By		(Signature of "Franking Officer.")			

TO — Essex Regt.

Sender's Number: *Bm: 1110   Day of Month: 1   In reply to Number: A A A

At 1100 there will be a rebombardment of German front line between (89) & point (03) aaa Bombardment ceases at 1230 - aaa Please continue your attack at 1230 on German front line between points (03) & (60)

From: 58th Bde.
Place:
Time:

The above may be forwarded as now corrected.   (Z)

Censor.   Signature of Addressor or person authorised to telegraph in his name.
* This line should be erased if not required.

"A" Form.
MESSAGES AND SIGNALS.
Army Form C. 2121.

Prefix	Code	m.	Words	Charge	This message is on a/c of:	Recd. at	m.
Office of Origin and Service Instructions.			Sent		Service.	Date	
			At	m.		From	
			To		(Signature of "Franking Officer.")	By	
			By				

TO { Essex Regt.

Sender's Number: Bm 1215
Day of Month: 1
In reply to Number:
AAA

The attack advance will take place at 12.45 instead of 12.30

From: 88th Bde
Place:
Time:

R. Wilson Capt.

The above may be forwarded as now corrected. (Z)
Censor. Signature of Addressor or person authorised to telegraph in his name.
* This line should be erased if not required.

"A" Form.   Army Form C. 2121.
MESSAGES AND SIGNALS.   No. of Message

Prefix	Code	m.	Words	Charge	This message is on a/c of:	Recd. at _____ m.
Office of Origin and Service Instructions.			Sent			Date 88 Bde
a24			At _____ m.		Service.	From 1/7/16
			To			
			By		(Signature of "Franking Officer.")	By

TO   all Battns

Sender's Number.	Day of Month	In reply to Number		AAA
G BM 170	1	-		

A barrage will be placed on enemy's front line from 10 pm till 10.30 pm tonight to allow of stragglers and wounded coming in. Strong parties will be organised by Worcs and Hampshires to help in wounded

From 88th Bde
Place
Time

"A" Form.   Army Form C. 2121.
MESSAGES AND SIGNALS.   No. of Message

Prefix	Code	m.	Words	Charge	This message is on a/c of:	Recd. at	m.
Office of Origin and Service Instructions.			Sent		Service.	Date	87 Bde
A2P			At ___ m.			From	1/7/16
			To		(Signature of "Franking Officer.")	By	
			By				

TO — all Bns (A2T)

Sender's Number: PM 1745   Day of Month: 1   In reply to Number: AAA

87th Bde. will form up for the collecting trenches & move forward between 10 & 10.30 troops in front of our firing line Please warn batteries

From: 88th Bde
Place:
Time:

The above may be forwarded as now corrected.   (Z)
Censor.   Signature of Addressor or person authorised to telegraph in his name.
* This line should be erased if not required.
(632) —McC. & Co. Ltd., London.— W 11400/2045. 100,000. 2/15. Forms C 2121/10.

"C" Form (Duplicate). Army Form C. 2123.
MESSAGES AND SIGNALS. No. of Message ....

JM FEPM 29 AZQ | Charges to Pay. £ s. d. | Office Stamp.
L/C Goody J | | AZT
 | | 1-7-16

Service Instructions.

Handed in at ..... AZQ ...... Office. 1825 m. Received 1826 m.

TO: ALL BATTALIONS

Sender's Number | Day of Month | In reply to Number | AAA
BM 1814 | 1st | |

Re my 1720 the barrage will be made on enemy's front line from 10:30 PM to 11:30 PM and not as therin stated

FROM PLACE & TIME: AZQ

Phone J Goody L/C

"C" Form (Duplicate).   Army Form C.
MESSAGES AND SIGNALS.   No. of Message

SM FHPM 21   AZQ   Charges to Pay.   Office Stamp.
    Sgt Kara J   £ s. d.   AZT
                2-4-16
Service Instructions.

Handed in AZQ .... Office 8.10 m. Received 8.56 m.

TO AZT

Sender's Number | Day of Month | In reply to Number | AAA
SC 1830 | 2ND | |

YBI estimates your present strength as 30 ~~four~~ or 488 please confirm or modify by return wire

FROM
PLACE & TIME   AZQ

J Karn Sgt.   Phone

"C" Form (Original).　　　　　　　Army Form C. 2123
MESSAGES AND SIGNALS.　　　　No. of Message ....

Prefix　Code　Words	Received	Sent, or sent out	Office Stamp.
	AZQ	At .... m.	AZT
£　s.　d.	From		2-4-16
Charges to collect	By J. Searing	To	
Service Instructions.		By 1650	1822

Handed in at ...AZQ...　　　　Office .... m. Received .... m.

TO　ALL BATTNS

*Sender's Number	Day of Month	In reply to Number	AAA

SS 1800　　2nd

Withington and Gabion avenue
closed to in down traffic
tonight

FROM　　AZQ
PLACE & TIME
　　J. Searing　　　　　　　Phone

	A" Form.				Army Form C. 2121.
	MESSAGES AND SIGNALS.				No. of Message

Prefix	Code	m.	Words	Charge	This message is on a/c of:	Recd. at	m.
Office of Origin and Service Instructions						Date	
			Sent		Service.	From	
			At	m.			
			To				
			By		(Signature of "Franking Officer.")	By	

TO	A 3 Q			
* Sender's Number.	Day of Month. 2nd	In reply to Number	A A A	
Your	S. 1830	our	present	strength
25	and	650.	This	includes
the	10 %.			

From
Place
Time

The above may be forwarded as now corrected.   (Z)

Censor.   Signature of Addresser or person authorised to telegraph in his name.
* This line should be erased if not required.

29th Division.

88th Infantry Brigade.

1st BATTALION

ESSEX REGIMENT

AUGUST 1 9 1 6

Confidential.

War Diary
of
1st Bn. The Essex Regiment.

From August 1st To August 31st. 1916

(Volume No. 17.)

Army Form C. 2118.

WAR DIARY
or
INTELLIGENCE SUMMARY.
(Erase heading not required.)

Place	Date	Hour	Summary of Events and Information	Remarks and references to Appendices
YPRES	1.8.16 to 7.8.16		Battalion in Brigade Reserve at YPRES. H.Q. Convent. Work Digging New X lines every night. Intermittent shelling in YPRES itself. 1st Bttn rejoined from Reserve, and took over command of "X" in place of Capt Powell.	
	8.8.16		Gas attack by Germans. Gas reached cellars in YPRES, for which wore by every one, also no man affected by the gas. Our artillery put a moderately heavy barrage on enemy front line. Germans did not attack.	
FIRING LINE	9.8.16 to 11.8.16		Relieved Hants Regt in left of RAILWAY. W coy from DUKE STREET to PARK LANE. Z coy from PARK LANE to left of X3 line. Y coy in support in X2 line. X coy in reserve in X3 line. Trenches in bad condition & suffer from attention. Frequent work done both by day and night, mostly in filth & crates. Germans made a raid on 115 far B, F, of 10 to 12 men, one German got into our trench by the GULLY, and bombed our men Wheatley & Pte Edwards, all three died. The German belonged to the M.L. 362 Regt, 2nd in clear but in addition which a no my fresh in part of W coy line. 2nd Lt. McLean died of wounds at 10th Casualty Clearing Station. One German captured by Capt Paton.	
	12.8.16			

1st Batt. Essex Regt.

WAR DIARY
or
INTELLIGENCE SUMMARY

Army Form C. 2118.

Place	Date	Hour	Summary of Events and Information	Remarks and references to Appendices
Firing line	13.8.16		The casualty of rgng'l to 16th Bgde machine gun trying along our front line. Pte Perry who died of wounds 2cas, Pte O. Skilled but artillery retaliation was effective in stopping it. Three men slightly wounded in 2cas.	
	14 P.M.		X coy relieved W coy in firing line. Y coy relieved Z coy. Relief carried out without event. Extra work to be done in fully augmented trenches of comrades has proven an arduous time out. "Erato". D.H.Q.s Picard ely. Communicated trenches, also trench from calm to railway by no plk.	
	15.8.16 to 17.8.16		Relieved by 16th Middlesex. Relief not completed until 2.45am on 19th marched to YPRES by platoons and entrained all the battalion in O'Camp by 5a.m.	
O'Camp	20.8.16 to 25.8.16		Battalion training for assault at arms. Gas helmet drill, Phyical training and close order drill. Assault at arms with Battalion won three events.	
	26 P.M.		(1) Consolidation of strong point. (a) Relay Race. (3) Cross country Race. (4) Inter Coys Competition	

Army Form C. 2118.

1st Batn. Essex Regt.

WAR DIARY
or
INTELLIGENCE SUMMARY.
(Erase heading not required.)

Instructions regarding War Diaries and Intelligence Summaries are contained in F. S. Regs., Part II. and the Staff Manual respectively. Title pages will be prepared in manuscript.

Place	Date	Hour	Summary of Events and Information	Remarks and references to Appendices
O. Camp	27.8.16 to 29.8.16		In 'O' Camp carried on with Coy and Pln drills and pos defence in trenches. Lt. Tomlinson joined from 3rd Essex. Rated G.Zog.	
	29.8.16		On the night of 29/30th moved up into the firing line and relieved the 16.15th Middlesex Regt. in X.2 & X.3 firing line Yeo in support and X coy in reserve at X.3. Took over the Camel Lines Bivouac.	
	30.8.16		During relief gas alarm sounded which afterwards turned out false. Very heavy rain, reaction floods in fact many A.W O3 lines wet. Can Flaig evacuated to hospital. Woke I from Pen up Pln not dispirited	
Firing line	31.8.16			

[signature] Lieut Colonel

Commanding 1st Bn. Essex Regiment

29th Division.
88th Infantry Brigade.

1st BATTALION

ESSEX REGIMENT

SEPTEMBER 1 9 1 6

Confidential.

War Diary
of
1st Bn. The Essex Regt.

from 1-9-16 to 30-9-16.

(Volume 18)

Army Form C. 2118.

1st/3rd ESSEX REGT.

WAR DIARY
INTELLIGENCE SUMMARY.
(Erase heading not required.)

Place	Date	Hour	Summary of Events and Information	Remarks and references to Appendices
TRENCHES.	1.9.16. to 3.9.16.		Very wet weather, work carried on as usual, chiefly drainage. Gas alarms, which were found out to be false, hindered work. Party a good deal, especially owing to preparations having to be made in case our own gas was let off. Y coy. relieved W. coy. in firing line, and X coy. relieved Z coy. in firing line on night of 3rd/4th. W coy. went to A Posts and Z coy. in reserve in X 3 and Potije defences.	
	4.9.16. 5.9.16. to 7.9.16.		Work hindered by more gas alarms. Patrols went out and examined wire, weather cleared, and trenches were drained, where needed. A good deal of shelling by french mortars, mostly in the Gully and Crater, our artillery retaliation was not effective. O. mart. of 14th Chesh. were sent to relieve with	
	8.9.16.		On the night of 8th/9th Battalion was relieved by Harts. Regt. and went into Brigade Reserve in YPRES. We have slightly wounded.	
YPRES.	9.9.16. 10.9.16. 11.9.16. 12.9.16. to 15.9.16.		Diggings day and night, chiefly R.E. fatigues. Diggings carried on, reduced fatigues for carrying materials. Working parties carried on as usual. Diggings and carrying parties, days and nights.	

WAR DIARY

INTELLIGENCE SUMMARY

Army Form C. 2118.

1/5th Essex Regt.

Place	Date	Hour	Summary of Events and Information	Remarks and references to Appendices
YPRES.	16.9.16 to 18.9.16		DICKEBUSCH huts as usual. One of the huts was heavily shelled by enemy 8 inch mortars. The result being, the hut was blown in and we had 4 killed & 9 wounded.	
D'Camp	19.9.16		Battalion was relieved by the 1/6th Middlesex Regt. and went into reserve in 'G' Camp. Relief took place without incident.	
	20.9.16 to 27.9.16		At 'G' Camp. Digging every third night 370 men & seven officers. Capt. & Quarter Master acquainted to 10 CCS broken collar bone. 2Lt. R.F. Sheddle joined the Battalion from 9th Res. Trench. Bn. Battalion were though the gas charge, with her as companion and felt no ill effects. Training carried on as far as possible.	
YPRES	29.9.16		Moved to YPRES and went into same billets as before. HQs in Convent in divisional reserve. Relief carried out without incident.	
	30.9.16		In YPRES no report. digging every 6: carrier. Nº 86" 487" 16 Bobn.	

Wallinger Lieut Colonel
Commanding 1st Bn Essex Regiment

29th Division.

88th Infantry Brigade

1st BATTALION

ESSEX REGIMENT

OCTOBER 1 9 1 6

CONFIDENTIAL

War Diary of

1st Bn The Essex Regiment

From 1st October 1916   To 31st October 1916

(Volume 19)

WAR DIARY
INTELLIGENCE SUMMARY
(Erase heading not required.)

Army Form C. 2118.

Instructions regarding War Diaries and Intelligence Summaries are contained in F.S. Regs., Part II. and the Staff Manual respectively. Title pages will be prepared in manuscript.

Place	Date	Hour	Summary of Events and Information	Remarks and references to Appendices
YPRES	1.10.16 to 4.10.16		In Divisional reserve in YPRES. Dyson's Baths reduced owing to mine explosion. Handed over stores and equipment to 9th Kings Liverpool Regt.	
YPERINGHE	5.10.16 to 7.10.16		Moved by train to Poperinghe. In billets in Poperinghe. Instruction and battalion training, no training carried out Daily. Entrained at Hopoutre for Longpré 10.30 pm - 1.00 a.m. 8 th. Train journey lasted 10 hours.	
CORBIE	8.10.16 9.10.16		Marched to CORBIE from LONGPRÉ. 10 mile march. Moved in lorries two turns to camp S.26.c. and camped in the open for the night.	
TRENCHES	10.10.16 & 11.10.16		Battalion marched up to the support line through DERNAN: Wood. Relieved this 6th West Kent Regiment, companies in the following manner: W Coy. GIRD TRENCH. X + Y Coys PIONEER TRENCH Z + HQ in BULL'S ROAD. Moved up with C Coy to firing line as Co. Cd. In position by	

WAR DIARY
or
INTELLIGENCE SUMMARY

Place	Date	Hour	Summary of Events and Information	Remarks and references to Appendices
TRENCHES	12.11	2 am to 12th inst.	W and X Coys. in front line in front of GUEUDECOURT, Y and Z Coys in support in SUNKEN ROAD. Two front line companies fought continuously & got into two report line continually consolidating and forming their at 2.30 p.m. W & X Coys fought to advanced their own damage and took 1st objective following by Y and Z coys. On gaining 1st objective, half Z Coy went on to Eaucourt reinforcing X Coy. Remainder of Y and Z Coys swung left handed as first objective. These had not been gained by 7th Suffolk Regiment. They came under heavy shell fire and machine gun fire and endeavoured to dig in. Shell holes. The attack here was held up and White Corps commander ordered 9.30 p.m. when this returned and organised on our original front line. Meanwhile W & X companies dealt with Germans in dugouts on a first objective killing about 300 and capturing 60 Germans. This Bttn advanced from 1¼ to 2½ objectives (approximately)	

WAR DIARY
INTELLIGENCE SUMMARY.
(Erase heading not required)

Army Form C. 2118.

Place	Date	Hour	Summary of Events and Information	Remarks and references to Appendices
TRENCHES	12.10.16		and at about half way came under heavy machine gun and rifle fire from front and flanks. At about the front 15 Germans appeared from a dug out and shewed signs of surrender. One German however jumped on Lt. Eastwood who shot him. North the two companies Lt. Eastwood came up and shortly after him also, the remainder of the Germans were then killed. Both Company commanders, Capt. Forbes and Lt. Carolin then found that they had not got enough on either flank and were unable to advance. These two companies then gradually retired in where they reorganised and then took to original front line where they were to 1st Objective. Battalion relieved by 11th Worcester Regiment and kept in PIONEER TRENCH, Y and Z Coys + BUCKS ROAD	
	13.10.16 to 14.11.16		Y and Z Coys moved out to new firing line at LT TRENCH, W Coy took over the original front at head of BREDECOURT X Coy in support on SUNKEN ROAD. Confused sniping was the principal occupation until 17.11.16. Trenches extremely wet and deep	

WAR DIARY

INTELLIGENCE SUMMARY
(Erase heading not required.)

Army Form C. 2118.

Place	Date	Hour	Summary of Events and Information	Remarks and references to Appendices
TRENCHES	16.10.16		were received a good deal of attention from our artillery to the the result that several casualties occurred.	
	17.10.16		Y and Z Coys moved to PIONEER TRENCH. W Coy remained up in the old firing line. X Coy moved into HUNT TRENCH in its entirety.	
	18.10.16		Moved up 15th & 16th attack were by H/Q 6 cooks and 2 stretcher bearers Reg. Details very wet and windy.	
	19.10.16		H.Q. returned to BULLS ROAD, leaving Z Coy in jumping off trenches in front of W Coy. H.Q. was in BULLS ROAD.	
	20.10.16		W Coy and Z Coys that relieved its BULLS ROAD on morning 20th ult. Weather too also very wet and poor covered in mud. The men were all very done up. Battalion was relieved by K.O.S.B. Reported and gone by Platoons to BERNAFAY CAMP, Devil Clare 88 bottles by 3 pm. On the way down 2 Lt. Claud and C.S.M. Cole killed and Lt. Brigade H.Q. Battalion went into bivouacs in a advance Brigade H.Q. Remainder in Camp, working chiefly on officers in tents.	

WAR DIARY

INTELLIGENCE SUMMARY

Place	Date	Hour	Summary of Events and Information	Remarks and references to Appendices
BERNAFAY CAMP	24/10/16 25/10/16 26/10/16		roads, and burying dead horses. Baxter and Lewis evacuated. Carried out training as fairs as possible. Men refitted with clothing etc. Weather very wet and dull/foggy. No shells in the vicinity, two bombs were dropped from an aeroplane doing no damage. Relieved 16th Batallion Pyramids for night. 9th + 8th Brigade in line of FISHS. Y and Z Coys in support, W and X Coys in supports to Bath HArb. Find two Coys and dffy rept and one Coy and one Coy Trench Mortar batts into and vctm Coys to right. Batallion relieved by 14th Australian Brigade in relief proceeded to BERNAFAY Camp one stage the night, HQ moved from BERNAFAY Camp to MAMETZ VILLAGE on rout into huts there.	
BERNAFAY CAMP	30/10/16			
MAMETZ CAMP	31/10/16		Batallion marched to MERICOURT-L'ABBÉ and arrived there at 2pm and went into billets.	302/f EB Wardham Lt. Colonel Cmdg 1/Border Regt

1/Essex October 1916

O.O. No 13. 10/10/16

The Bn will relieve the W. Kents in support
Parade 4.20 PM Fighting Order.
Great Coats will be worn.
Officers Kits & packs with waterproof sheets
will be stacked by Coys in T. Lines by
8.30 PM Mess tins will be carried
Water bottles will be filled
Guides will conduct the Coys to their position
Coys will move at 100 yds between platoon
in the order HQ W X Y Z.
On arrival at position Coys will detail
two guides to report at Bn H Q. These
guides will then return to Camp & report
to the Staff Capt at Divl. Canteen near
T. Lines. They will then conduct the
ration party by pack transport to a
Regtl Dump shown by the Staff Capt.
Tools Bombs etc will not be drawn from
1st Line but taken over from W Kents
Regtl Dump.
10% will be taken & further orders
regarding these will be issued

(Sgd) G.R.S. Drage /
  Bn

I. The first & second platoons will be fighting platoons. Bombers will be included in these.

II. The third platoon in each Coy will be the consolidating platoon & each man will carry either (i). Pick or shovel
(ii). Corkscrew or barbed wire
(iii). Wire cutters 6 per Platoon
2 sandbags per man.
Lewis Gunners will be with the third platoon.

III. The fourth platoons will be the supporting platoons

IV. Coys to send in estimate immediately for what is required to complete.
These will be drawn by parties of 1 N.C.O. & 12 men per Coy who will proceed unarmed to Bde H.Q. at 11.30 am. Coys will be responsible that parties are sent to draw these stores at intervals until complete. Estimates to be sent to Bn H.Q at once.

11.10.16

(Sgd) G.V.S. Drowse Lt
a/Adj

Operation order no 19 In the Field
by Lt. Col. A. C. Halahan BULLS RD
Comdg 1st Essex Regt

Ref Sheet 57c S.W. 1/20,000 GUEDECOURT
2 trench maps. Oct 11th 1916

I The 88th Bde will attack on Oct 12th
Situation at an hour Zero and establish itself
on the Brown Line.

II The Essex Regt will take over the
Relief. left of the firing line from the New-
foundland Regt from N26B3.8. to
N26A7.10.

X & W Coys will take up a position in
the trench in front of Sunken road
Z & Y will take up position in Sunken
Road

The Right of X & Z will be in touch with
the N.F.L. Regt.
The left of W & Y will be in touch with
1st SUFFOLK Regt.

III The attack will be carried out as foll
Attack at Zero the artillery will put a

II.   A Barrage on the Green line & on Zone
II art. 200ᵡ in front when the leading lines
        will get forward as close as possible.
+6   At Zero + 6 the Barrage will lift
1st obj 100ᵡ beyond Green line & the leading
        lines will assault 1st objective.
+20   At Zero + 20 the leading lines will leave
2nd   Green line and advance at the rate
objective of 50ᵡ a minute to Brown line,
        which will be consolidated.
        Strong points will be constructed at
        C & D as detailed and patrols pushed
        forward.
III.   Companies will attack in 4 lines on
Formation a front of 2 Coys, each Coy on a front
of attack of 2 platoons
        W & X will be fighting Companies.
        Y & Z will be consolidating Companies.
        The Right of X & Z will be directed on
          pt N21 C 1.5 in green line and pt N 21 A 5.4.
        The left of W & Y will be directed on pt J 20 D 1.98
        in green line and pt N 14 D 5.1½ in
        Brown line.

IV contd. Bayonets will not be fixed until just before Zero.

V Reports. On reaching the red objective Brown line yellow flares will be lit, also at 7.0 am on 13th inst. in order to show positions to contact aeroplanes.
An advanced telephone, together with pigeons & a signal lamp will be established near pt N26B.1.9. Every endeavour should be made to send messages of situation to this point or to Batte H.Q.at ptN 26C 8.2.

VI Dressing Stations. Dressing stations will be established at points mentioned in V.

Dictated to O.C. Coys.
   O/C Lewis Guns
   O/C Bombers.
at 8.0 pm.
Dec 11th 1916.

12

Operation Orders.   Copy No 20
by M.W. Callaghan.

Ref. 1/10000.
1. The offensive will be resumed about
   dawn on Oct 18th. Zero will be
   notified later. The 88th Bde will
   advance & capture Grease Trench near
   pt N21 B2.2 a 3.8. to N20 D 6.9½ and
2. The attack will be carried out by the
   Worcestershire Regt on left and the Hampshire
   Regt on the Right.
3. At Zero the Artillery Barrage will be
   placed on BAYONET TRENCH & the
   Infantry will advance close behind the
   Barrage.
   The Barrage will then creep forward to
   to GREASE Trench & Infantry will
   assault
4. The Batts will be relieved on night
   of 17/18 & move as folls.
   HQrs & Y L 2 to BULL Rd.
        W Coy. to GIRD TRENCH.
        X Coy will remain in SUNKEN Rd

2. 4. cont. X & W Coys will be prepared to to occupy our present front line after the attacking troops have left it, on receipt of definite orders from Brigade Headquarters
i.e. X Coy to present W Coys line
W Coy to present Y & Z line.

5. Coys will detail carrying parties for rations, waters, &c at Bull Road at 6.30 pm tonight.
Also parties of 16 men to draw blankets at a point to be notified later after the relief has been carried out.

6. Coys will report when relief is complete.

G.A. Browne Lt
a/Adjt

17. 10. 16.

Addenda to Operation Orders No 20

1. O.C. X Coy will leave the post of 1 officer and 15 men & one Lewis Gun in the Gun pits in order to protect the left flank of the Worcestershire Regt against any possible counter attack during tomorrows operation.

2. Zero is at 3.40 am this is not to be given to anyone but the officers in charge of parties or platoon officers.

3. O.C. W will detail 1 officer (Lieut Lawson) & 25 other ranks
   O.C. Y will detail 1 officer (Lieut Read) & 25 other ranks
   to report to O.C. Divisional R.E. in GOAT TRENCH at 3.0 am tomorrow morning 18th inst. They will take the days rations with them.

   G V L Prowse Lieut.
   a/adjutant.

29th Division.
88th Infantry Brigade.

1st BATTALION

ESSEX REGIMENT

NOVEMBER 1 9 1 6

Confidential

War Diary of

1st Bn. The Essex Regiment

(Volume ~~20~~)

From 1:XI:16. to 30:XI:16.

Army Form C. 2118.

WAR DIARY
or
INTELLIGENCE SUMMARY.
(Erase heading not required.)

Instructions regarding War Diaries and Intelligence Summaries are contained in F. S. Regs., Part II. and the Staff Manual respectively. Title pages will be prepared in manuscript.

Place	Date	Hour	Summary of Events and Information	Remarks and references to Appendices
MERICOURT L'ABBE'	1-11-16 to 15		Battalion in rest billets. Company training and a practice attack carried out. Weather fine on the whole.	
MEAULTE	15-11-16 to 17-11-16		Under canvas in SANDPIT Camp 1000ˣ S.E of MEAULTE. Moved to TRONES WOOD	
TRONES WOOD	21-11-16	4:30 pm	"B" in bivouac employed in carrying material to front line Casualties 10. "B" went into firing line in relief of 4th WORCESTERS	
FIRING LINE	to 24-11-16		2 Platoons each of No 2 Coys in FALL TRENCH 2 " " " 9 " " AUTUMN " 1 " " " " " " " 3 " " " " " WINTER " "Z" Coy in COW TRENCH. Casualties 4.1.- all from shell fire, many appeared very nervous & put up frequent Verey lights. Relieved by 1st Royal Dublin Fusiliers	30 [signature]
" CARNOY	24-11-16 to 27-11-16	7 pm	On huts N.E. CARNOY.	
	27-11 & 2 "		Moved to bivouacs in TRONES WOOD & remained there till 30-11-16	
	30-11-16	7 "	Relieved 4th Worcesters in Firing Line	

[signature]
Lt Colonel Comdg 19th Eastern Div.

29th Division.

88th Infantry Brigade.

1st BATTALION

ESSEX REGIMENT

DECEMBER 1916

CONFIDENTIAL

WAR DIARY.

OF

1st Battalion The Essex Regiment.

From 1st December 1916 to 31st December 1916

(Volume)
~~20~~

WAR DIARY
or
INTELLIGENCE SUMMARY.
(Erase heading not required.)

Army Form C. 2118.

1 ESSEX

Place	Date	Hour	Summary of Events and Information	Remarks and references to Appendices
Firing Line	1-12-16		In front line in front of LES BOEUFS, very few casualties, Lieut Broomfield killed	
BERNAFAY	2-12-16		Relieved by R.Dublin Fusiliers + proceeded to BERNAFAY CAMP.	
CARNOY	3-12-16		Moved from BERNAFAY to CARNOY CAMP, 2/Lieuts Andrews & Hamilton joined	
"	4– 7-12-16		In CARNOY CAMP Resting	
BERNAFAY	7-12-16		To BERNAFAY CAMP	
Firing Line	8-12-16		In front line in front of LES BOEUFS, relieved 4th WORCESTERS, weak	
"	" 11		Very bad trenches in bad condition, Lieut Read killed	
"	11-12-16		Relieved by 11th Rifle Brigade & marched to Camp at CARNOY	
CARNOY	12 —		Entrained for VILLE	
VILLE	12/13 –		VILLE, Draft of 447 arrived, 2nd Lieut A. Pyim joined	
CONDÉ	14-12-16		Entrained for LONGPRES + reached same the evening	
MONTAGNE	15 —		Marched to MONTAGNE	
"	" 15 —		In MONTAGNE, Billets very [good]	
"	"		In Corps reserve at MONTAGNE	
"	31-12-16		Training	

30th
Essex

D.W.Man. Major H? 1st
Comdg 1/Essex Regt

VOLUMNE 23

CONFIDENTIAL.

War Diary
1st Battalion Essex Regt
From 1st January 1917
To 31st January 1917

1st Essex Regt.

WAR DIARY or INTELLIGENCE SUMMARY.

Army Form C. 2118.

1st ESSEX REGT.

Place	Date	Hour	Summary of Events and Information	Remarks and references to Appendices
MONTAGNE	11.7.17		Bn in Corps Reserve, training. Strength Officers 12 men 965. the following Officers joined from the Reinf. Lieuts Vickers, Knight, Osmondson, Macaulay, Nevill. Major Gunne rejoined.	
"	"		A.horses at AIRAINES 3pm Detamed CORBIE 6.30pm also Lieut GODDARD	
CORBIE	12.7.17		In billets CORBIE, Lieut Barker & 14 a/s & 100 o/ms	
"	13.7.17		Bryant CORBIE	
MEAULTE	"		Marched to MEAULTE	
MEAULTE	14		" Camp CARNOY	
CARNOY	17		" " GUILLEMONT. Lieut Sharpey joined	
GUILLEMONT	18		Relieved 1st R. INNISKILLING F. in left sector. Bn relieved front line F.O.H.	
Front Line	19		1 BENNETT, Twelve Casualties 1 other Burninker	
"	20		from trenches to camp GUILLEMONT	
CARNOY	21		Camp CARNOY	
"	22		To camp GUILLEMONT	
GUILLEMONT	23		GUILLEMONT	
"	24		Relieved 1st R.O.S. Borders, in A & G Batways & B. hd onps LINCOLN + MERCIER Trenches	

1st ESSEX REGT. Army Form C. 2118.

WAR DIARY
INTELLIGENCE SUMMARY.
(Erase heading not required.)

Place	Date	Hour	Summary of Events and Information	Remarks and references to Appendices
Front Line	25-1-17		Trenches. Lieut Wickes killed on patrol.	
	26 -		Relieved by R. INNISKILLING F.	
GUILLEMONT QUARRIES	27-1-17		Bn 2 Coys CARNOY. 2 Coys GUILLEMONT. Successful attack by BORDER + R. INNISKILLING on German trenches in front of LINCOLN + MERCIER Tr.	
GUILLEMONT	28		One Coy in Gen BOURIL Tr.	
	29		Relieved S. WALES BORDERS in left sector Bn moved FALL BENNETT	
	30			
	31		+ Neuve Captured LANDWEHR Tr. Casualties 7 wounded	

W Parker Captain
for O.C. 1st Essex Regt

Confidential

War Diary
of
1st Bn. The Essex Regiment
for
February 1917

(Volume 23.)

Army Form C. 2118.

WAR DIARY
or
INTELLIGENCE SUMMARY.
(Erase heading not required.)

1ST ESSEX REGT.

Instructions regarding War Diaries and Intelligence Summaries are contained in F.S. Regs., Part II. and the Staff Manual respectively. Title pages will be prepared in manuscript.

Place	Date	Hour	Summary of Events and Information	Remarks and references to Appendices
CARNOY	1-2-17		In Camp resting. Strength 21 officers & 65 other ranks	
GUILLEMONT	2-2-17		In Brigade reserve.	
	3-2-17			
Firing Line	4-2-17 to 6-2-17	7.30pm	Firing Line E. of LES BOEUFS from N35C.6.0 to N35C.6.4. Uneventful tour of trenches very quiet, but only a few casualties	
CARNOY	7-2-17 8-2-17	7.30pm	Relieved by 14th K.R.R. (20th Divn) & marched to CARNOY. Moved by bus to CARDONETTE	
CARDONETTE	9-2-17 to 18-2-17		In Billets. Training	
LANEUVILLE	19-2-17	10am	Marched to LANEUVILLE 6 kilmtres there for the night.	
	20 -	1pm	Entrained at CORBIE, detrained at PLATEAU & marched to FREGICOURT.	
FREGICOURT	21 - 22	8.30pm	In reserve in FREGICOURT. Left for firing line 7pm	
Firing Line	22/23-2-17	Midnight	In relief SAILLY-SAILLISEL Sector. Firing line consisted of isolated posts. Very uneventful	
FREGICOURT	24 - 25 -		Relieved by 4th Worcesters & march to FREGICOURT	
BRONFAY	25-26 -	10am	Marched to TRONES WOOD & entrained, detrained PLATEAU, marched to BRONFAY, Brigade reserve.	
COMBLES	27 - 28		Marched to COMBLES & remained there. Left for front line 5pm.	6582

Officers joining during month, 2nd/Lt EYRE, TURK, McDONALD, Lieut B.O.LMER.C.
Strength 33 Officers, 814 other ranks

A.W.Tym Capt.
for Lt Col. Halahan
1st Essex Regt.

2353   Wt. W2544/1454 700,000 5/15 D. D. & L.   A.D.S.S./Forms/C. 2118.

Confidential.

659L
813

War Diary
of
1st Bn The Essex Regt
for
March 1917.
(Volume 25)

WAR DIARY

INTELLIGENCE SUMMARY

1st ESSEX REGT.

Army Form C-2118

(Erase heading not required.)

Place	Date	Hour	Summary of Events and Information	Remarks and references to Appendices
Firing Line	1-3-17		SAILLY - SAILLESEL Sector, Strength 33 Officers, 854 other ranks, Casualties 3 men	
FRICOURT	2		Relieved by 4th Worcesters. On relief went into reserve in dugouts in FRICOURT.	
BRONFAY	3		Marched to TRONES WOOD & entrained for BRONFAY Camp, arrived BRONFAY 2 pm	
BRONFAY	4-5-6		Marched to huts MEAULTE.	
MEAULTE	18th		Training for open warfare.	
	19th	7am	Arrived at EDGE HILL. Attained at HANGEST thence by march route to	
			MONTAGNE LE FAYEL arriving 1.30 pm	
MONTAGNE	20th-28th		Training for open warfare.	
PICQUIGNY	29th	1pm	Marched to PICQUIGNY billeting there for night	
FLESSELLES	30th	9am	Marched to FLESSELLES	
"	31st		FLESSELLES. Strength 31 Officers, 892 other ranks	

Confidential.

War Diary
of
1st Bn The Essex Regt
for
April 1917
(Volume 26)

Army Form C. 2118.

WAR DIARY
or
INTELLIGENCE SUMMARY.
(Erase heading not required.)

Instructions regarding War Diaries and Intelligence Summaries are contained in F. S. Regs., Part II. and the Staff Manual respectively. Title pages will be prepared in manuscript.

Place	Date	Hour	Summary of Events and Information	Remarks and references to Appendices
FLESSELLES	1.4.17		Strength : 31 Officers 892 other ranks.	
	2.4.17		Left FLESSELLES at 11 am. Arrived BEAUVAL 3pm, billeted for the night.	
MONDICOURT	3.4.17		Left BEAUVAL 8.30 am. Arrived MONDICOURT 1pm. Went into huts.	
	4.4.17		Training	
	5.4.17		Training	
			Left MONDICOURT at 2.30pm for IVERGNY, arriving 6.30pm.	
IVERGNY	6.4.17			
	7.4.17		Left IVERGNY at 11 am for HUMBERCOURT arriving 1pm.	
HUMBERCOURT	8.4.17		Training	
	9.4.17			
	10.4.17		Left HUMBERCOURT at 11 am for FOSSEUX arriving 2pm. Billeted in huts.	
FOSSEUX	11.4.17			
	12.4.17		Left FOSSEUX at 7.30 am arriving in ARRAS 3.30pm. Went into line at MONCHY-LE-PREUX.	
Line	13.4.17		MONCHY - LE PREUX.	
	14.4.17		Attacked German line at 5.30 am. Casualties 17 Officers 644 other ranks.	
	15.4.17		Remainder of Batt went into CAVES in ARRAS at 8pm.	

Army Form C. 2118.

WAR DIARY
or
INTELLIGENCE SUMMARY.
(Erase heading not required.)

Instructions regarding War Diaries and Intelligence Summaries are contained in F. S. Regs., Part II. and the Staff Manual respectively. Title pages will be prepared in manuscript.

Place	Date	Hour	Summary of Events and Information	Remarks and references to Appendices
ARRAS	15.4.17		In Corps Reserve	
	16.4.17		" "	
	17.4.17		" "	
	18.4.17		" "	
	19.4.17		Went into BROWN LINE near MONCHY	
	20.4.17		In BROWN LINE, Composite B^n of ESSEX & NEWFOUNDLAND Regts	
	21.4.17		" "	
	22.4.17		" "	
	23.4.17		Relieved and billeted in BARRACKS in ARRAS.	
	24.4.17		Left ARRAS at 7pm by bus arriving at SIMENCOURT at 9pm	
	25.4.17		SIMENCOURT.	
	26.4.17		Left SIMENCOURT for GOUY at 11am, arriving at 1pm	
	27.4.17		Left GOUY at 9.15am arriving at BAYEN COURT 2pm	
	28.4.17 to 30.4.17		BAYENCOURT. In training.	

(Temporary) War Diary
of
1st Bn. The Essex Regt.
for
April 1917
(Volume 26)

88th Bde

This is only a temporary measure.
The proper diary is unfortunately at
COUTOURELLE dump.
It will be forwarded on the first opportunity.

Sidney J. Tune Maj.
1st Essex Regt

2/5/17

Army Form C. 2118.

April 1917. WAR DIARY
or
INTELLIGENCE SUMMARY.
(Erase heading not required.)

Instructions regarding War Diaries and Intelligence Summaries are contained in F. S. Regs., Part II. and the Staff Manual respectively. Title pages will be prepared in manuscript.

Place	Date	Hour	Summary of Events and Information	Remarks and references to Appendices
FLESSELLES	1st		Left FLESSELLES at 11am by march route arriving BEAUVAL at 3pm en route to join Maj. Genl. Trevor's 16th Corps. The Army of Pursuit. Strength 31 officers and 792 O.R.	
	2nd		Left BEAUVAL 8.30am arrived MONDICOURT at 1pm. No men fell out on this somewhat trying march and the C.O. was complimented by G.O.C. 88th Bde. on the good marching of the Bn.	
			MONDICOURT.	
	3rd & 4th			
	5th		Left MONDICOURT 2.30pm arrived IVERGNY 6.30pm	
	6th		IVERGNY.	
	7th		Left IVERGNY 11am arrived HUMBERCOURT 1pm	
	8th & 9th		HUMBERCOURT.	
	10th		HUMBERCOURT to FOSSEUX.	
	11th		FOSSEUX	
	12th		The Bn marched from billets at FOSSEUX to ARRAS (alt 10 miles) and on arrival was at once ordered to proceed with the remainder of the 88th Bde to relieve the 37th Batt near MONCHY-LE-PREUX. The Bn arrived at ARRAS at 3pm and left to carry out the relief 4 miles off at 6.30pm. Owing to intense congestion on the road and other delays relief was not completed until 3am on 13th. Prior to leaving ARRAS orders had been issued for an attack on the German line in company with the 1st NFLD	

WAR DIARY
or
INTELLIGENCE SUMMARY

(Erase heading not required.)

Army Form C. 2118.

Place	Date	Hour	Summary of Events and Information	Remarks and references to Appendices
			to be made on the 13th at an hour to be notified later.	
			The attack was to be made from an assembly trench which was to be dug on the night of the 12/13 by 2nd Hants. 4th Worcs were in support to the attack.	
			Owing to the late hour at which the Brigade relief was completed & consequent impossibility of making adequate preparation for the attack the operation was postponed.	
			At daylight therefore on the 13th the Brigade was ordered as shewn in the attached map.	
			At 11am orders were received to make the attack at 2pm. These orders also were cancelled a few minutes before Zero.	
			During the night 13/14 the 2nd Hants dug the required assembly trench and operation orders were issued to H/2nd by Lt Col Halahan	App 3
			At 5:30am on 14th the barrage fell and the battalion left the trench & carried out the assault. In spite of a certain weakness of the barrage the objective was gained and by 6:30am all companies had reported that they were busy digging in.	
			In the meantime "D" Coy detailed to form a flank guard to the three attacking Coys were at once come in contact with the enemy. Therefore acting under Capt Foster's orders No. 5 Platoon got into shell holes at about O.15.B.1. and	

WAR DIARY
or
INTELLIGENCE SUMMARY
(Erase heading not required.)

Army Form C. 2118.

Place	Date	Hour	Summary of Events and Information	Remarks and references to Appendices

opened fire. No 5 Platoon being checked by machine gun fire from ARROW COPSE No 7 was directed to outflank this copse with the result that No 8 could again get forward, capturing the 2 machine guns entering the enemy end of the copse. The small wood at O 2 a 7.5 was also meanwhile occupation sent was cleared by Lewis Guns & rifle grenades. The company then moved forward to the N end of the copse where all platoons came under fire from a line of hidden machine guns. The company now proceeded to form the chain of strong points as detailed in operation orders. From this point no further definite news could be gathered as to the fate of this company. A few men eventually rejoined the battalion & from their statements it is certain that all Platoons reached their proper positions where they were at once attacked by very superior German forces were finally overwhelmed in their positions at a time between 6.30am and 7.30am.

The main attack by the remaining 3 Coys having reached the objective by 6.30am started to dig in and reports were sent back to Bn Hqrs that large forces of the enemy could be seen in the BOIS du SART & R 313 and AUBE PIN E3 and that all covering parties sent forward, were at once coming under heavy machine gun + rifle fire. It became apparent rapidly to the Coy Commanders that an immediate counter attack was being prepared and this was also reported to Bn Hqrs. These reports were confirmed by two Coy Commanders in person returning wounded from the main attack.

Steps had already been taken to get the Artillery on to the points where the enemy was reported to be massing but

Capt Jackman
Capt Carter

Army Form C. 2118.

WAR DIARY
or
INTELLIGENCE SUMMARY.
(Erase heading not required.)

Place	Date	Hour	Summary of Events and Information	Remarks and references to Appendices
			owing to the destruction of the wires by shell fire it was an hour before the guns opened fire. By 7.30am the counter attack had fully developed in all its strength & at least 9 Battalions. The weight of the attack appears to have come from the N East & Ransfeld on 2nd Coy. This Coy in spite of a stout resistance was gradually overwhelmed. From 7.30 onwards scraps of parties, messages or wounded men arrived at Btn Hqrs at the Red Post 1A in Kayrine apparent that 'C' Coy having been overrun the whole force got between MONCHY & the attacking companies of the Essex & NFLD. No men have returned from these companies. As soon as it became clear that MONCHY itself was being attacked patrols were put out from the Hqr party to hold their barricades in MONCHY. No Germans succeeded in entering MONCHY. It must be remembered that during all this time the town was under an intense enemy barrage. Also preventing it almost impossible to reinforce or support the two Battalions & making the work of the respective Hqr parties extremely arduous. Except for a certain amount of support from the 4 Worcester & 2nd Hants they fought in line & these two Battalions broke up a German attack designed not to drive them back but to retake MONCHY itself. Appendix C contains a copy of the Special Order issued by the G.O.C. 37 Bde. Officers who went into action the following be killed : 2/Lt L. Cowan The following are wounded : Capts R&Q Bardin, J Donkinson Lucks D.W.J. Taylor	War App. C.

2353   Wt W2514/1454   700,000   5/15   D. D. & L.   A.D.S.S./Forms/C. 2118.

WAR DIARY or INTELLIGENCE SUMMARY

Army Form C. 2118.

Place	Date	Hour	Summary of Events and Information	Remarks and references to Appendices
R. Ecolivert			The following are missing:- Capt H.J.B Dolin, Lt C.R. Brown, 2/Lt A.L. Piper, 2/Lt R. Byrne, 2/Lt Orwin, 2/Lt Hunt, P/O Coombs, L.J. Portway; P/O Dark.	
	15th		Total casualties 17 officers + 644 O.R. out of a strength of 31 officers + 892 O.R.	
	16th		The remnants of the Battalion were now withdrawn & went into billets in ARRAS.	
	19th to 22nd		A draft of 125 O.R. from an entrenching battalion of the Essex Regt. was received. A composite battalion made up of the Essex & Newfoundland Regts took over the "Brown Line" & were employed there in putting that line in a state of defence & on various working parties in connection with the operations then going on.	
	23rd		The composite Battalion was relieved & returned to ARRAS.	
SIMENCOURT	24th		Capt K.M. WEARNE and G.C. GIBSON reported for duty from England. Lt Col A.C. Nalahn left on this day to take command of the 29 Divisional Details his place being taken by Lt Col Sir George Stirling Bt. D.S.O.	
SIMENCOURT	25th			
GOUY	26th			
BAVINCOURT	27/30		The training & reorganisation of the new draft was now taken in hand.	

Confidential.

War Diary
of
1st Bn. The Essex Regt.
for
May 1917.
(Volume 27)

WAR DIARY
or
INTELLIGENCE SUMMARY.

(Erase heading not required.)

Army Form C. 2118.

Place	Date	Hour	Summary of Events and Information	Remarks and references to Appendices
BAVINCOURT	15/1/17		By this date the battalion had been reorganised and the two drafts sorted out although very short of officers and specialist NCOs. 2 Lieuts Lyon Kearn per coy and Manning joined. 21/1/17 Major Kneed O/R. was in process of formation when orders was received to move to SAULTY. The battalion now 21 officers & 414 O.R. strong marched over 12 in charge of SAULTY 11C on	Stamp
	2.5.17		Left SAULTY by rail ?? train for ARRAS	
ARRAS	3.4.16		In billets on the Grande Place, ARRAS. During these days the battalion found fan. of its	CAPT. E.C. BURGES
		6.15	companies for forward Besides continuing the training of the men the whole of it	A.F. BOWSHER 21.4.17 DRAFT
			which were sent if the has spent extended tins of material	Draft 202
	1.5.17		The battalion was withdrawn to BERNEVILLE	Draft
			Yesterday these officers managed joined, and 16 joined for duty on the date	SCARP
	8.1.17		Training at BERNEVILLE	VAR
	10.5		Marched from BERNEVILLE to ARRAS	BLAK
	11.5.17		Billets in ARRAS	
	12.5.17			
	14.5.17			
	1/7		Occupied BROWN LINE about NEW establ.	

WAR DIARY
or
INTELLIGENCE SUMMARY.
(Erase heading not required.)

Army Form C. 2118.

Place	Date	Hour	Summary of Events and Information	Remarks and references to Appendices
	May 14th		Relieved the Royal West Kents on the left sector of the Divisional front in the neighbourhood of ORANGE HILL	
	21st		Relieved the 2nd Hants and Rifles on the BROWN line about N.28 c.x.c	
	25th		Relieved 1st NFLD in the intermediate line about N.36	
	27th		Relieved the 1st NFLD in the same sector of the front line as before	
	31st		Strength on 31.5.17 "F" officers x 651 O.R.	
			Thus period calls for no special comment. No units entered the intermediate sector if there was not fire under fire. The battalion was under shell fire of varying degrees of intensity during the whole period and suffered the undermentioned casualties	
			Lieut. R.O. WARNER killed 19.5.17	
			Capt. R.M. WEARNE)	
			Capt. M.A. CHAWNER) killed 21.4.17	
			Lt. M.C.W. KORTRIGHT)	
			Other ranks Killed 12. Wounded. 45	

Confidential

War Diary
1st Essex Regt

From 1st June 1917 To 30th June 1916

(Volume No. 28)

(Volume 27.) 1st Bn. The Essex Regt. Army Form C. 2118.

WAR DIARY
or
INTELLIGENCE SUMMARY.

From 1st June 1917 to 30th June 1917.

(Erase heading not required.)

Instructions regarding War Diaries and Intelligence Summaries are contained in F. S. Regs., Part II. and the Staff Manual respectively. Title pages will be prepared in manuscript.

Place	Date	Hour	Summary of Events and Information	Remarks and references to Appendices
ARRAS	June 1st		In the trenches. Heavy bombardment on Devil's Trench by our heavies.	
"	2		" Great Artillery and Aircraft Activity. We had a few casualties	
"	3		Relieved from trenches by King's Liverpool Regt.	
"	4		Proceeded to Cellars in Grand Place ARRAS.	
"	5		Entrained at ARRAS for Montelet. Arrived Candas & Marched to Montelet	
MONTRELET	6		Training.	
"	7		"	
"	8		"	
"	9		"	
"	10		"	
"	11		"	
"	12		"	
"	13		"	
"	14		"	
"	15		"	
"	16		"	

WAR DIARY
or
INTELLIGENCE SUMMARY.
(Erase heading not required.)

Army Form C. 2118.

Place	Date	Hour	Summary of Events and Information	Remarks and references to Appendices
MINTRELET	17		Training	
,,	18		,,	
,,	19		,,	
,,	20		,,	
,,	21		,,	
,,	22		,,	
,,	23		,,	
,,	24		,,	
,,	25		,,	
,,	26		,,	
,,	27		Marched to DOULLENS, entrained for HOPOUTRE, detrained at HOPOUTRE, marched to PROVEN.	
PROVEN	28	9 p.m.	X. Y v Z Coys. entrained & marched to RIVELD FARM for working on YSER Canal	
,,	29		Working on YSER.	
,,	30		X.Y.Y Coys returned by Rout March to PROVEN. W Coy moved from PROVEN to RIVOLI	
			W & Z Coys bivouaced at RIVOLI preparing working parties on the Yser Canal.	

2353 Wt. W2544/1454 700,000 5/15 D. D. & L. A.D.S.S./Forms/C. 2118.

Confidential

War Diary
of
1st Bn The Essex Regiment
For month of July 1917.
(Volume 29)

Army Form C. 2118.

WAR DIARY
or
INTELLIGENCE SUMMARY.
(Erase heading not required.)

Instructions regarding War Diaries and Intelligence Summaries are contained in F.S. Regs., Part II. and the Staff Manual respectively. Title pages will be prepared in manuscript.

Place	Date	Hour	Summary of Events and Information	Remarks and references to Appendices
E. of PROVEN	1st July 1917 to 4th		Strength :- 23 Officers 830 other ranks. 13th (less 2 Coys) in Camp just E. of PROVEN. Two Coys at RIVOLI F.M (B 24 Central) employed on work under R.E.	
S.E. of EYKHOEK	5th 6th		13th (less 2 Coys) marched to Camp "H" S.E. of EYKHOEK.	
L.2 Defences	7th to 9th		Left Camp "H" 7.45 pm and marched to "L 2" Defences (B 23 a). Owing to heavy shelling on ELVERDINGHE - BRIELEN Rd. had to march by circuitous route. Arrived L 2 Defences 11.30 pm. No casualties. Were joined there by remaining two Companies.	
L.2 Defences In the Line	10th		In L.2 Defences supplying working parties for R.E. and digging new support to front line. Relieved 4th Worcesters in Right Sub-Sector C. 13 b. Line held with 2 Coys: in firing line + 2 in support. Very little shelling in front line, but 13th H.Q.rs on Canal Bank continuously shelled with 5.9 and 8" Armour piercing. Casualties very light.	
S.E. of CROMBEKE	12/13th 14 to 18 19th		Relieved by 2nd Royal Fusiliers and marched via Crackes (?) to Camp S.E. of CROMBEKE arriving 3am In Camp training for forthcoming offensive.	
S. of HARINGHE	20th		Marched to Camp immediately S. of HARINGHE.	

WAR DIARY
or
INTELLIGENCE SUMMARY.
(Erase heading not required.)

Army Form C. 2118.

1st Essex Regt

Place	Date	Hour	Summary of Events and Information	Remarks and references to Appendices
S. of HARINGHE	July 21/22		In Camp training.	
	23rd		Left camp 5am. Marched to training ground at HERZEELE for a day's Brigade training. Returned to camp at 7pm. Only two men fell out after this day's 14 hours work.	
S.E. of CROMBEKE	24th		Returned to camp S.E. of CROMBEKE.	
DE WHIPPE CABARET	25th		Relieved 1st Bn Grenadier Guards at DE WHIPPE CABARET.	
	26/28		Attached Guards Div. carrying material for the approaching attack up to front line. Heavy barrage put up continuously during night caused many casualties to carrying parties. A few men gassed by new gas known as "Mustard Gas". Casualties: 1 Officer. 35 other ranks.	
S.E. of CROMBEKE	29th		Marched to camp S.E. of CROMBEKE.	
" "	30/31		In camp in reserve to Guards Division. Strength 25 Officers 812 other ranks.	

Grant Stirling
Lieut. Colonel
Commanding 1st Bn Essex Regiment

Confidential

War Diary

of

1st Bn The Essex Regt

for

August 1917.

(Volume 30)

Army Form C. 2118.

Instructions regarding War Diaries and Intelligence Summaries are contained in F. S. Regs., Part II. and the Staff Manual respectively. Title pages will be prepared in manuscript.

WAR DIARY
or
INTELLIGENCE SUMMARY.
(Erase heading not required.)

Place	Date	Hour	Summary of Events and Information	Remarks and references to Appendices
	1.8.7.		In camp S.E. CROMBEKE in Corps reserve to Guards Division.	
	2nd	3.50am	Guards Division attacked. Weather fine. Guards Division reported to have gained all their objectives	
		6.30pm	Heavy rain which continued throughout the day & night.	
	3rd-5th		Training – Bad weather still continued.	
	6th	11am	Marched to a camp in wood W. of DE WIPPE CABARET arriving 1pm.	
	7th	6.30pm	Marched to camp S.E. WOESTEN arriving 7.30pm.	
	8th		In Camp.	
	9th		Left camp 5.15pm & relieved 16th Middlesex in left support line.	
	10th		Heavy enemy shelling – very few casualties.	
	11th		Relieved by 1st Border Regt. Relief complete by 11.30pm arrived in camp W. of DE WIPPE CABARET about 2am.	
	12th		In camp practising for the coming attack.	
	13th	2.30pm	Marched to camp S.E. WOESTEN.	
	14th		In camp practising for attack.	
	15/16th		Bn Bt - strength 17 Officers 585 other ranks - left camp at B.H.Q. at 7.30pm proceeded by track 12 to BOESINGHE. Owing to rain, going was fairly heavy. Arrived BOESINGHE about 9.10pm and proceeded via HUNTER ST. Duck boards to position of assembly, in the open S. of River STEENBEEK our night starting on	

WAR DIARY or INTELLIGENCE SUMMARY

Army Form C. 2118.

Instructions regarding War Diaries and Intelligence Summaries are contained in F. S. Regs., Part II. and the Staff Manual respectively. Title pages will be prepared in manuscript.

(Erase heading not required.)

Place	Date	Hour	Summary of Events and Information	Remarks and references to Appendices
	10/16		The Railway. Owing to darkness & rough state of ground, cut up by shell fire & tapes leading to position of assembly being more too clearly laid, a certain amount of congestion & confusion arose, parties losing their way etc.	
		3.45am	B". was in position. The enemy had apparently seen or heard units moving & he kept up a steady barrage throughout the night, but although the whole Brigade was lying in the open there were very few casualties – the hostile barrage going well over their heads.	
			The plan of attack was in conjunction with 20th Division on right & French on left to capture the RED & intermediate lines.	
			The Division attacked with 2 Brigades – 88th Bde on right, 87th Bde on left, 86th Bde being in reserve.	
			The frontage & objectives are shown on attached map.	
			The 2nd Hants & 1st Newfoundland Regt attacked the BLUE & GREEN lines & the Essex and 4th Worcestershire Regts the RED line.	
			After Zero the Hants & Newfoundland pushed forward 2 Coys across the river. The remaining 2 Coys of these Bns remaining on the S. side further up as close to the river as possible. The Essex & Worcesters being immediately in rear.	
		4.45am	At Zero 4.45am barrage opened & all crossed to far side, each Bn having 4 foot bridges	

Army Form C. 2118.

WAR DIARY
INTELLIGENCE SUMMARY.
(Erase heading not required.)

Place	Date	Hour	Summary of Events and Information	Remarks and references to Appendices
	16"		to cross. All got safely across on far side before enemy barrage fell & formed up in same formation here. At 4.50 am the barrage commenced to move forward at rate of 100yds in 5 minutes. The enemy opened a heavy barrage, but fortunately this was on a line well S. of the STEENBEEK. The 13th followed up the HAMPSHIRE REGT. keeping in artillery formation & maintaining touch with the Worcesters on left & 11th. Duke Cornwall's Light Infantry on right.	
		4.50 am		
		6 am	At 6 am. The GREEN Line was captured. The Cooks passed through the Hampshire Regt. & at 7.45 am. practically to the time table. Assaulted & captured the RED LINE. During the advance from the GREEN Line to the RED Line the right Company "W" encountered and dealt with four enemy strong points, those along the Railway Line & one on their left taking 20 prisoners and killing some Germans. The left assaulting Company engaged the enemy's snipers who were holding up the advance of the Worcesters a little, and enabled the Worcestershire Regt to continue their advance without losing their barrage. When the RED LINE was assaulted a few Germans held out, but practically all the garrison still left alive came forward as soon as the barrage permitted surrender "W" Company's Commander then pushed forward according to instructions previously	

2353 Wt. W2544/1454 700,000 5/15 D. D. & L. A.D.S.S.:Forms/C. 2118.

WAR DIARY
INTELLIGENCE SUMMARY

Army Form C. 2118.

Place	Date	Hour	Summary of Events and Information	Remarks and references to Appendices
	16th		given him & captured the huts at U.17.c.65.20. killing some of the garrison & capturing 23 more prisoners.	
			"X" Coys Commander consolidated a strong point at U.16.d.9.3. & captured 30 prisoners amongst the ruins at this point.	
			The Left support Company pushed forward a platoon to fill a gap between "X" & "W" Coys in the German line taking 18 prisoners.	
			The right support Company Commander finally occupied the German front line or "W" moving forward into the German service trenches & the huts at U.17.c.60.20. In all some 170 prisoners were taken, 6 machine guns, & 1 trench mortar. The 6 Machine Guns were taken over by the 88th M.G. Coy.	
			"W" & "X" Coys then pushed forward patrols to the BROENBEEK & ascertained that none of the enemy were South of that line.	
		9 am.	At 9 am. a party of 12 Germans, one mounted, were seen at U.16.b.8.4. They scattered into shell holes on "X" Coys firing at them & the rider made off to GRUY TERZAELE Farm close by.	
		10 pm	At 10 pm patrols sent out to the BROENBEEK reported all clear, but a patrol from "X" Coy at 11.30 pm	

Army Form C. 2118.

Instructions regarding War Diaries and Intelligence Summaries are contained in F. S. Regs., Part II. and the Staff Manual respectively. Title pages will be prepared in manuscript.

WAR DIARY
INTELLIGENCE SUMMARY.
(Erase heading not required.)

Place	Date	Hour	Summary of Events and Information	Remarks and references to Appendices
			encountered a hostile patrol of 8 men at U16d 8.4 (South of the BROENBEEK) and killed two bringing back prisoners the third.	
		1am	At about 1 am the relief of the 13th commenced. All day long hostile artillery fire was very active on our front line. Contact planes arrived according to time table, but for the rest of the time our front line was much harassed by low flying enemy planes. The front line was visited about 2-3pm by the commanding officer. — there were at least five or six flying low over our line & reconnoitring it quite unhindered by any of our air craft. The whole terrain was a mass of water filled shell-holes & the effort to cross it entailed the supreme determination of the men. One cannot speak too highly of the spirit and gallantry of all ranks — whilst the way in which successive strong points were tackled and covering fire to flanks was afforded, reflects the greatest credit on both the officers who trained them & the men who carried out the operations. Throughout the day, those holding the front line were intermittently exposed to our own artillery fire, & it was with difficulty that the strong point at U17c65 20 was maintained by a double garrison in a block house.	

WAR DIARY
INTELLIGENCE SUMMARY.
(Erase heading not required.)

Army Form C. 2118.

Place	Date	Hour	Summary of Events and Information	Remarks and references to Appendices
	16th		In the attack the 13th suffered the following Casualties:- Killed. A.D. McDonald & A.P.H. Davison. Wounded, 122 other ranks killed, wounded & missing.	
	14/7 17th		Relieved by 2nd 13th the Royal Fusiliers. Relief completed by 5 am 17th.	
	18th		In Work 18. E. of BOESINGHE. Heavily shelled. Casualties - 6.	
	19th		Moved to Camp at BOESINGHE.	
	19/20/21/22		Relieved 1st 13th Lancashire Fusiliers in right support. In right support in newly captured sector. Continuously shelled. Casualties - Captain D.S. Robertson (R.A.M.C. attached) wounded, other ranks 7 killed, 22 wounded. Relieved by Royal Inniskilling Fusiliers. Relief completed 11.30 pm. Marched to Camp just N. of ELVERDINGHE.	
	24th		Marched to camp W. of DE WIPPE CABARET.	
	25-26		In Camp.	
	27th		Marched to PRIVET Camp N.E. of PROVEN.	
	28th		Marched to PUTNEY Camp. N.E. of PROVEN.	
	6/31st		In Camp refitting & training.	

Ernest Stanley /Lt.
Cmd 1/4 Suss. Regt.

CONFIDENTIAL.

WAR DIARY

OF

1st Bn. ESSEX REGIMENT.

From 1st September 1917   To 30th September 1917.

VOLUME No. 31.

Army Form C. 2118.

WAR DIARY of 1st Batt. ESSEX REGT.
for month of SEPTEMBER
or
INTELLIGENCE SUMMARY.

(Erase heading not required.)

Place	Date	Hour	Summary of Events and Information	Remarks and references to Appendices
PUTNEY CAMP	1917. Sept 1st		Battalion at rest. Training	
ditto	2nd		ditto	
ditto	3rd		ditto	
ditto	4th		ditto	
ditto	5th		Brigade Ceremonial Parade at which Major General Sir Beauvoir de Lisle Commanding the Division presented medals & decorations to the officers NCOs & men who had distinguished themselves in August 16th. the following officers NCOs & men of the Battalion were awarded Distinctions.	
ditto			Capt. D.S. Pilton RAMC MC (absent wounded) No. 41447 Sgt W Hunt MM	
ditto			Capt E. C. Rushworth MC " 16493 " W Redburg MM	
ditto			Lieut J W Rouse MC " 44534 Pte F Harper " "	
ditto			O C Price MC " 3821 Sgt A Barrington MM (absent wounded)	
ditto			No. 41573 Sgt P Russell DCM " 9325 Cpl H Cusson MM (absent wounded)	
ditto			" 9678 W/CpL R Jones DCM " 9574 Cpl J Eligely MM (absent wounded)	
ditto			" 34903 Sgt E Soster MM " 34809 Pte W South MM (absent died of wounds)	
ditto			" 9769 Pte L Chapman MM " 34839 " A Prescott MM (absent wounded)	
			" 34882 " J Clinver " (absent wounded)	

WAR DIARY
or
INTELLIGENCE SUMMARY.
(Erase heading not required.)

Army Form C. 2118.

Instructions regarding War Diaries and Intelligence Summaries are contained in F.S. Regs., Part II. and the Staff Manual respectively. Title pages will be prepared in manuscript.

Place	Date	Hour	Summary of Events and Information	Remarks and references to Appendices
PUTNEY CAMP			The following NCOs were also decorated for bravery in putting out a fire caused by hostile aircraft fire on	
ditto			the CANAL BANK on July 16th	
ditto	Sept 6th		9110031 Sgt W Smith M.M. 14825017 Cpl. J Steed M.M.	
ditto	" 7th		Battalion at rest training	
ditto	" 8th		ditto	
ditto	" 9th		ditto	
ditto	" 10th		ditto	
ditto	" 11th		ditto	
HERZEELE	" 12th	2p.m.	Battalion marched to HERZEELE training area	
ditto	" 13th		On leave training practising the attack	
ditto	" 14th		ditto	
ditto	" 15th		Brigade Day on which the brigade practised the attack	
ditto	" 16th		Battalion marched back to PUTNEY CAMP	
PUTNEY CAMP	" 17th		Battalion at rest training	
ditto	" 18th		ditto. There was a Competition for the Drums from to all regiments in	

Army Form C. 2118.

WAR DIARY
or
INTELLIGENCE SUMMARY.
(Erase heading not required.)

Instructions regarding War Diaries and Intelligence Summaries are contained in F. S. Regs., Part II. and the Staff Manual respectively. Title pages will be prepared in manuscript.

Place	Date	Hour	Summary of Events and Information	Remarks and references to Appendices
PUTNEY	1917		The Corps in which the Divn. & the 1st Essex Regt. was came under the 1st Bde.	
CAMP	Sept 19th		Battalion at post training	
ditto	20th	11am	Entrained at PROVEN for DULWICH CAMP the 3rd who were not going into the line left the	
			Battn. at ELVERDINGH STATION for BEDFORD CAMP in that Cpl. GRANT.	
DULWICH CAMP	21st		Battalion absorbed the 3rd reinforcement furnished guides to the right sub-sector of the Divisn. at front	
in the line	22nd		Holding the line. X & Z Coys in the right front line, Y Coy on the right bank the right on the STADEN	
ditto	23rd		RAILWAY. Z Coy on left in touch with the 1st Battalion WORCESTERSHIRE Regt & W Coy in support, X Coy in REVEUR	
ditto	24th		in support, W Coy in REVEUR. Was considerable enemy shelling two first & second line trench. Patrolling was carried out nightly, important the enemy establishing themselves	
ditto	25th		on the south side of the BROEMBEEK which is probably in support of the 2nd & 3rd Brit. W.M.	
ditto			GARVIN and shelled by a sniper. Camouflage some fairly heavy especially in the support & reserve	
ditto			lines which required a considerable amount of gas shells, 9th until & clock August 7 C. DINAN	
ditto			2nd Lieut. E. PEARSON was severely... Total casualties during the tour in the line were 3 Officers 141 O.Ranks.	
ditto	25th		Battalion was relieved in the line by the 2nd Battln. HAMPSHIRE Regt. & returned to DULWICH	
ditto			CAMP	
DULWICH CAMP	26th		Battalion at rest training	

WAR DIARY
or
INTELLIGENCE SUMMARY.

(Erase heading not required.)

Army Form C. 2118.

Place	Date	Hour	Summary of Events and Information	Remarks and references to Appendices
DULWICH CAMP	Sept 23rd 1917		Battalion at rest training	
ditto	" 26th	2 pm	Battalion marched to "H" Camp	
H. Camp	" 29th		Battalion at rest training. Major F.C Dwyer died at 6.9 pm from the effects of gas.	
ditto	" 30th		ditto	

CONFIDENTIAL

WAR DIARY

OF

1st/5. ESSEX REGIMENT

FROM 1st October 1917 TO 31st October 1917.

(VOLUME No. 32)

WAR DIARY of 1st/13th Essex Regt.

or

INTELLIGENCE SUMMARY.

(Erase heading not required.) From 1/10/17 to 31/10/17

Army Form C. 2118.

Instructions regarding War Diaries and Intelligence Summaries are contained in F. S. Regs., Part II. and the Staff Manual respectively. Title pages will be prepared in manuscript.

Place	Date	Hour	Summary of Events and Information	Remarks and references to Appendices
Suez	1		Repairing 1st & 11th Infantry tracks.	
	2		Training. A party of 8 Offrs & 200 O.R. marched to BOESINGHE at 2 a.m. & returned in the same evening having buried 250 yards*	*& others in big inst. 200 O.R.
	3		Training & repairing 1st & 11th Infantry track.	
	4		Training. A fatigue party of 6 Offrs & 200 O.R. employed on work which extended on big inst.	
	5		Training & repairing 1st & 11th Ind. track.	
	6		The Battn marched to CARIBOU CAMP, leaving "H" CAMP at about 11.30 am	
	7		W & X Coys moved to CANAL BANK & provided carrying parties for carrying 16 battles stores to an advanced dump	
	8		The Battn less W & X Coys moved to the CANAL BANK & occupied the dug-outs which the 1st Newfoundland Regt had vacated. Verbal orders for the attack at 1.45 a.m. Lt. A. Fatigue parties carried material forward to the attack.	
	9		The 13th entrained at ELVERDINGHE; detrained at INTERNATIONAL CORNER & marched to SUEZ CAMP, arriving at about 12 midnight. Parties had been carrying ammunition etc. to the new front line during the day.	
	10th & 15th		Training	

2353 Wt. W2544/1454 700,000 5/15 D. D. & L. A.D.S.S./Forms/C 2118.

SHEET 2

WAR DIARY of 1st/13th ESSEX REGT

Army Form C. 2118.

INTELLIGENCE SUMMARY. From 1/10/17 to 31/10/17.

(Erase heading not required.)

Place	Date	Hour	Summary of Events and Information	Remarks and references to Appendices
	16		Left SUEZ CAMP at 3 p.m. & marched to PESEHOEK & entrained at 6.30 p.m. Arrived at SAULTY at 9.30 a.m. 17th & marched to billets in POMMIER arriving at 12.30 p.m.	
	18th to 31		Training in POMMIER area.	

Ernest Stirling Lt Col.
Comdg 1st/13th Essex Regt.

1.XI.17

CONFIDENTIAL

WAR DIARY

OF

1st BN. ESSEX REGIMENT

FROM 1st NOVEMBER, 1917 TO 30th NOVEMBER, 1917

(VOLUME NO. 33)

Confidential

War Diary
of
1st Bn. The Essex Regt
for
November 1917.
(Vol. 33.)

Army Form C. 2118.

WAR DIARY
or
INTELLIGENCE SUMMARY.
(Erase heading not required.)

Instructions regarding War Diaries and Intelligence Summaries are contained in F.S. Regs., Part II. and the Staff Manual respectively. Title pages will be prepared in manuscript.

Place	Date	Hour	Summary of Events and Information	Remarks and references to Appendices
POMMIER.	Nov 1.11.17		At Pommier. Presentation by G.O.C. 29th Division of medals for operations on October 9th.	
POMMIER.	2nd to 16th		Training.	
	17th		Left Pommier, marched to BOISLEUX au MONT and entrained. Detrained at PERONNE and marched under cover of darkness to MOISLAINS.	
	18th		Left Moislains at 6.30 pm and marched to SOREL le GRAND.	
	19th		In order to ensure concealment of operations men were kept in huts during the day.	
	20th	2.0 am	The Battalion marched to places of assembly W. of GOUZEAUCOURT arriving at 4.40 am. At 6.30 (Zero hour) the battle was commenced by the Divisions advancing in lines preceded by lines of tanks of which in this operation some 200 were employed. Their objectives were the 1st & 2nd trenches of the HINDENBURG LINE on the capture of which the two outer divisions were to form defensive flanks to the advance of the 29th Division. The task assigned to the 29th Division was to push through the St QUENTIN Canal, seize the crossings at MARCOING and MASNIERES and then allow the cavalry to go through to CAMBRAI. At 6.30 am the Battalion moved to the forming up area about FARM RAVINE (R.20.a.) and at 8.45 am the Companies moved off to take up their positions as advance guard to the 88th Brigade. "Y" Coy: forming the Vanguard in the first Captured German Line, the other Coys: in our old front line. The	

Place	Date	Hour	Summary of Events and Information	Remarks and references to Appendices
	20th	9.20 am	was emptied by 9.20 am. At 11 am the advance was sounded by bugle and the Battalion went forward, "W" Coy on the right, "Z" Coy on the left & "X" Coy in support. The four tanks preceded the Vanguard, themselves guided by eight Battalion scouts; all Coys in Artillery formation until the 2nd Objective was passed, when they extended into two lines. Opposition was first encountered from a strong point about L.36.d. just beyond the HINDENBURG Support line and this strong point was captured at 12 noon, 7/o prisoners being taken. Lieut Davies was wounded by a Machine shot during the surrender of the prisoners. Shortly after this a platoon under Captain Hobday captured three field guns and two machine guns were also taken in the strong point. Enemy troops still held the outskirts of LES RUE VERTES South of Masnieres but was soon dislodged by the combined operations of the ESSEX and WORCESTERSHIRE Regiments. At 11pm the Canal was reached, but unfortunately the bridge which had apparently been prepared for destruction collapsed under the leading Tanks hereby blocking all advance, and the advance was subsequently held up by heavy Machine Gun & Rifle fire from Masnieres on the Northern side of the Canal. In spite of all efforts to get across under covering fire from S.O.S. limbers no progress was possible at this point and the southern bank of	

WAR DIARY or INTELLIGENCE SUMMARY

Army Form C. 2118.

Place	Date	Hour	Summary of Events and Information	Remarks and references to Appendices
	20th		The Canal was accordingly lined by troops under whose covering fire efforts were made to cross by one or two foot bridges. Under cover of the fire from platoons of Y & W Coys Capt Bretton, crossing a small foot bridge, established his company in a mill on an island between the river and the Canal and endeavoured by his fire to cover further attempts to cross. At 4.30 p.m. by the aid of 2 tanks which gave covering fire, Lieut Marchant with some of his men made a gallant attempt to rush a small pontoon bridge, but was killed with several of his men in the effort. Further gallant attempts were made by Capts Mattison commanding Y Coy. and Lieut Hepgrave with small parties, but without success, both of these Officers being killed & Lieut Rice wounded with many of his men. It was therefore decided to cease these efforts & organise the defence of the Canals for the night. In the meantime the Lock bridge in L.24.d. to the West and another at G.27. to the East had been secured by the NEWFOUNDLAND and WORCESTER Regts and who effected crossings at these points. A number of cavalry were in LES RUE VERTES like a sale dar in the hope of being able to get across, but were then withdrawn, a small party actually crossing by the lock bridge in G.27. At 11 p.m. mopping up parties from all four battalions were sent North of the Canal to clear out the snipers, a party of Coys under	

Army Form C. 2118.

WAR DIARY
or
INTELLIGENCE SUMMARY.
(Erase heading not required.)

Instructions regarding War Diaries and Intelligence Summaries are contained in F.S. Regs., Part II. and the Staff Manual respectively. Title pages will be prepared in manuscript.

Place	Date	Hour	Summary of Events and Information	Remarks and references to Appendices
	26th		Lents: Bungey, Hope and Vaughton co-operating with the Newfoundlanders in clearing up to the main MASNIERES - CAMBRAI Road. They returned at 3 am reporting all clear. Under orders received from Brigade to form a bridge-head, Y and Z Coys moved off at 3.45 am to cross by the lock at L.24. and establish themselves along the Railway G.19 central, G.20 central. At 4 am "Four Mills" (Intelligence Officer) set out with some scouts to reconnoitre the positions selected and at 5.30 am returned and reported that finding the enemy in occupation, Y & Z Coys had dug in along the Railway about his central in touch with Newfoundland Regt on their left. At 9 am W Coy was sent off ordered by the Intelligence Officer with instructions to establish themselves in rear of Y & Z Coys, to send patrols across to the East of the Cambrai Road and, should the front brigades of the MASNIERES - BEAUREVOIR line be found unoccupied by the enemy, to establish themselves therein. It was notified that at 11 am a combined attack by the 69th & 88th Brigades would advance and capture the MASNIERES - BEAUREVOIR line. At 11.50 am W Coy was held up West of the Cambrai Road and engaged the enemy, having found it impossible to get scouts across the Cambrai Road. At this junction Cambrai appeared to be moving in an Easterly direction	
	27th			

Army Form C. 2118.

WAR DIARY
or
INTELLIGENCE SUMMARY.
(Erase heading not required.)

Place	Date	Hour	Summary of Events and Information	Remarks and references to Appendices
	21st		from MARCHING along the ridge L.24 Central, G.19 Central leading the attack of the 87th Brigade. W Coy attempted to advance parallel to this Corps in a North Easterly direction but on reaching the Romer Line G.20 b. they were stopped by a cross machine gun fire and being unable to progress further formed a line on the Southern edge of the ridge in prolongation of the South Wales Borderers. There were many casualties from the heavy enemy fire and 2nd Lieut. Vaughton was reported "missing" after this action. Meanwhile at 10.5am Headquarters and X Coys started up the main Cambrai Road through Masnieres with a view to taking up their position in front of the Romer Line about G.20 d.5.8. to G.21 C.2.6. However on reaching the point G.20 d.6.5. they came under heavy machine gun and rifle fire from houses on both sides of the road and several rifle fell. Headquarters and X Coy opened a hot fire on the buildings from which the sniping came and under cover of this were withdrawn to the West of the village where their orders did not admit of delay. At 11am the attack of the 87th Brigade commenced and having failed to get its Non appointed position East of Cambrai Road, Headquarters and X Coy co-operated with the 87th Brigade covering their right flank during the advance. When the advance of the 87th Brigade ceased held up by resistance	

WAR DIARY
or
INTELLIGENCE SUMMARY
(Erase heading not required.)

Army Form C. 2118.

Place	Date	Hour	Summary of Events and Information	Remarks and references to Appendices
	21st		On the Cambrai Road, Headquarters marched, accompanied by X Coy via the Canal bank to a position near the sugar factory G.27.a., got in touch with Brigade H.Q. and awaited further orders. At 3pm. fresh units returned to Headquarters and reported the situation of the other 3 Coys. At 6pm orders were received to take up a position on the left of the HAMPSHIRE Regt. between the MASNIERES-RUMILLY and MASNIERES-CAMBRAI Roads about G.21.d.27., G.20.b.61 in touch with South Wales Borderers on the west of the Cambrai Road. Whilst this position was being reconnoitred and a tape got out four huts was despatched to the west of Masnieres to bring up W.Y. and Z Coys and by 7:30pm all Coys were in position digging in. Casualties on the 20th/21st amounted to - Killed, 3 Officers, 21 men; Wounded, 2 Officers, 107 men; missing 1 officer, 31 men.	
	22nd		The line occupied on the 21st was maintained until 6pm when the B[tn] was relieved by a B[tn] of the LANCASHIRE FUSILIERS and marched to Marcoing where it went into billets.	
	23rd		In billets & dugouts at MARCOING. On the afternoon of the 24th the Battalion was so heavy that the whole B[tn] was moved into one big dugout.	

WAR DIARY
or
INTELLIGENCE SUMMARY.
(Erase heading not required.)

Army Form C. 2118.

Instructions regarding War Diaries and Intelligence Summaries are contained in F. S. Regs., Part II. and the Staff Manual respectively. Title pages will be prepared in manuscript.

Place	Date	Hour	Summary of Events and Information	Remarks and references to Appendices
	25th	6 p.m.	The 18th relieve the INNISKILLING FUSILIERS in trenches N.W. of Marcoing.	
	26th		Previous night spent in developing a position and digging a strong point of situation normal except for good deal of machine gun fire.	
	27th		Situation normal. A few casualties from Artillery & machine gun fire.	
	28th		Situation normal. Relieved at 5.30 p.m. by INNISKILLING FUSILIERS, returning to Marcoing.	
	29th		Town heavily shelled all day.	
	30th		The day opened with heavy bombardment with Gas shells lasting from 7 to 9 a.m. A heavy German Counter attack having driven in the Division on our right. At 10 a.m. the 18th was ordered to assemble on ground to the South of Marcoing Copse. Owing to very heavy shelling, Headquarters & Coys proceeded independently, choosing their own routes. By 10.30 a.m. H.Q. had arrived at L.29 Central and 4 Coy had already advanced from that part Southwards against the Enemy some of whom had reached the sunken road immediately South of Marcoing Copse but were now retiring again Southwards leaving a number of dead, wounded and	

WAR DIARY
or
INTELLIGENCE SUMMARY
(Erase heading not required.)

Army Form C. 2118.

Place	Date	Hour	Summary of Events and Information	Remarks and references to Appendices
	30th		prisoners in our hands. W and Z Coys arriving shortly afterwards were ordered to prolong the line Eastward & join up with the Newfoundlanders who were forming a defensive flank facing S.E. about 4.30 a.m. At this moment Capt: Godard (the Adjutant) was wounded and Captain Bolding who had taken over Y Coy: was being brought back mortally wounded. During the advance of W and Z Coys, Capt Haws, commanding Z Coy was killed and Lieut Dicens severely wounded. As fighting was becoming severe, and much ammunition was (being expended), parties were sent down from B": HQ. to the outskirts of Marshaing to bring up ammunition and took it up to the front line. Several trips were made and tools were also sent up. HQ. now being themselves in at L.29 Central and Brigade HQ established themselves at L.28 d.5.7. About 3 p.m. X Coy who had been in reserve was pushed up to a position just East of BHQ. in L.29 central where they dug in. The Hampshires which was also in the line was withdrawn into Brigade reserve and the remaining units of the Brigade were ordered to reorganise and dig in; Worcesters on the right, Essex in the Centre & Newfoundlands on	

WAR DIARY or INTELLIGENCE SUMMARY

Army Form C. 2118.

Place	Date	Hour	Summary of Events and Information	Remarks and references to Appendices
	30th		left. A good line of strong points was therefore established along the line & points L35.b.0.2. and afterwards linked into a continuous trench and during the night a small amount of rations & water & much ammunition was sent up to them. Casualties during the evening of the 30th - Killed 1 Officer, 14 men; Wounded 4 Officers (1 mortally), 60 men; Missing 31 men.	

Ernest Stirling
LT-COLONEL
COMDG. 1st BN. THE ESSEX REGT.

Confidential

War Diary

of

1st Bn. Essex Regt

From 1st Decr 1917. To 31st Decr 1917.

(Volume No. 34)

WAR DIARY

1st Bn The Essex Regt.

Army Form C. 2118.

INTELLIGENCE SUMMARY.

(Erase heading not required.)

Summary of Events and Information

December 1st In action at MARCOING after Counter attack of 30th

At 6 a.m more rations arrived at Brigade Headquarters and were sent up to the Companies in the line. There was very heavy shelling on MARCOING COPSE and around Battalion Headquarters in the early morning until 8 a.m when it died down and at that time, the situation in our trenches was reported quiet. At 9.30 a.m Lt.Col Harrison at Battalion Headquarters and reported that having become aware of the enemy attack, he Joined some troops of the 6th Division who having been driven back were making a stand in a sunken road on the right of our line and had succeeded in driving the enemy backward. Heavy shelling continued all day on NINE WOOD and MASNIERES At 5 p.m. "Z" Company on the left reported that the enemy had been seen advancing over the ridge on their left front in large numbers but had been stopped by their fire. At 7 p.m it was reported that MASNIERES was in the hands of the enemy. The night passed quietly and at 11.30 p.m rain fell heavily

December 2nd. This morning the rain having ceased. In the early hours there was again heavy shelling behind our line and along the Canal. Several squadrons of

Army Form C. 2118.

WAR DIARY
INTELLIGENCE SUMMARY.
(Erase heading not required.)

Place	Date	Hour	Summary of Events and Information	Remarks and references to Appendices
	1917 December 2nd (Cont'd)		Enemy aeroplanes flew over our lines during the morning and one squadron of our planes crossed our line about 10 a.m. During the afternoon a very heavy enemy barrage was placed on NINE WOOD. The Hampshire Regiment was ordered to dig a reserve line, and two battalions of the 87th Brigade were relieved by another Division. There was no shelling in our front line but Annesnoille Machine Gun fire and Sniping. Companies were ordered to dig listening posts in front and support trenches behind the front line and during the night this was successfully carried out and by the morning an excellent system of trenches was completed.	
	December 3rd		The morning shews over his fire from 10.30 a.m. a heavy bombardment commenced on the General Bank and MARCOING COPSE which lasted for an hour. At 1.15 p.m. orders were sent to "X" Company to reinforce a Strong Point held by the Newfoundland Regiment just South of the MASNIERES – MARCOING ROAD and the Strong Point was being very heavily shelled at the time. At 2.15 p.m. one Platoon of the Worcestershire Regiment arrived to support "X" Company in place of the Platoon sent up. At 2.30 p.m. Captain Price of "X" Company was ordered to get	

WAR DIARY or INTELLIGENCE SUMMARY

Army Form C. 2118.

Place	Date	Hour	Summary of Events and Information	Remarks and references to Appendices
	1917 December 3rd (Cont'd)		in touch with the Newfoundland Regiment and reinforce at once if the situation demanded it. At 2.45 p.m. 3000 rounds S.A.A. were forwarded by us from Brigade to Newfoundland Regiment. At 3.15 p.m. the Platoon of "X" Company which had been in support of "Z" Company was sent to support the South Wales Borderers Regiment on the left of the Newfoundland Regiment and Captain Price and the Headquarters of "X" Company proceeded to take their place. Another Platoon of the Worcestershire Regiment was sent to occupy the support trench. At 3.50 p.m. orders were received for the Trench Mortar Batteries to fire on the enemy and in front of the Newfoundland Regiment strong point and then moved on of our line to a.a.a. till 9.30 p.m. Orders were received to await withdraw from our line to a position in rear. Arrangements were made for parts to the left of the line firing Very Lights till 5.30 a.m. the following morning the remainder to cover arrival in rear to the Hampshire Regiment reported "All clear" at 10.40 Our men were sent to bring back ammunition from the Machine Gun positions.	
	1917 December 4th.		At 1.30 a.m. 13 Battalion Headquarters left their old Headquarters and moves to a dug out in a sunken road behind the new line. 2.30 a.m. the Essex	

WAR DIARY
INTELLIGENCE SUMMARY

Army Form C. 2118

Place	Date	Hour	Summary of Events and Information	Remarks and references to Appendices
	1917 December 4th (Cont'd)		Regiment was reported "All clear". 5.45 am posts were withdrawn and at 6.30 am all were in their new positions. The morning opened quiet. Enemy aeroplanes flew very low, trying to spot our new line, and later a squadron of our own aeroplanes flew over the enemy lines. The situation of the Battalion was now as follows :- "X" and "Y" Companies were attached to the Hampshire Regiment, on the the left. "Z" Company was occupying a Strong Point, and "W" Company was dug in under a bank in the surroundings in support. At 2.30 pm the Commanding Officer of the 9th Royal Irish Fusiliers (36th Division) arrived at Battalion Headquarters and discussed relieving the Battalion later. At 4.45 pm orders were received for the relief. At 6.45 pm [strikethrough] "W" and "X" Companies were moved to dig the new line of posts. The Essex Regiment and Hampshire Regiment forming "B" line, the Commanding Officer of the Essex Regiment. This was commenced at 11.50 pm. Meanwhile "Y" and "Z" Companies were relieved, the line until the new Relief posts were completed.	

WAR DIARY
or
INTELLIGENCE SUMMARY.
(Erase heading not required.)

Army Form C. 2118.

Place	Date	Hour	Summary of Events and Information	Remarks and references to Appendices

1917 December 5th

At 4.30 am the relief was reported complete and Battalion Headquarters moved O/B arriving at RIBECOURT at 4 am. Here hot soup was provided from the cookers. At 8am the Battalion marched O/B as men and arrived at ETRICOURT at 10.30 am. Here a hot meal was provided and at 5.30 pm the Battalion entrained, though owing to the time being altered the train did not start until 10. pm. At 10.30 pm the train stopped suddenly owing to the engine having been hit by a shell and knocked O/B the track. After waiting for 1200 hours another train was brought up about 700 yards beyond the place where the rails were broken and all stores were transferred to the new train.

1917 December 6th. At 4.30 am the new train moved O/B and arrived at MONDICOURT at 4.30 am. Here hot cocoa was provided and at 11 am the Battalion marched to S.U.S. St. LEGER arriving there at 1 p.m.

1917 December 9th to 14th. Here we received two drafts of about 120 new recruits undergoing training.

1917 December 18th left SUS St. LEGER 9.40 am and marched to FLERS arriving at 4. pm

2353 Wt. W2544/1454 700,000 5/15 D. D. & L. A.D.S.S. Forms/C. 2118.

Army Form C. 2118.

WAR DIARY
or
INTELLIGENCE SUMMARY.
(Erase heading not required.)

Instructions regarding War Diaries and Intelligence Summaries are contained in F. S. Regs., Part II. and the Staff Manual respectively. Title pages will be prepared in manuscript.

Place	Date	Hour	Summary of Events and Information	Remarks and references to Appendices
	1917 December 19th		At 8.30am the Battalion left FLERS and marched to WAMBERCOURT arriving at 5.30 p.m.	
	1917 December 20th		At 10.30am the Battalion left WAMBERCOURT and marched to ROYON arriving at 3.0 p.m.	
	1917 December 21st to 31st		Here the Battalion underwent training and received two drafts one of 30 men and one of 60 men various other reports were here. Xmas day was spent very successfully the Battalion being provided with roast pork and Christmas puds up for their dinner and General Monts Weston arrived to see the men who served under him in Gallipoli.	

Cuyf... [signature]
for
LT.-COLONEL,
COMDG. 1st BN. THE ESSEX REGT.

Herewith war diary of 1st Batt ESSEX
REGT. for month of January, 1918.
Please acknowledge receipt.

F. Hopson 2/Lt.
for
Brigade Major
88th Inf Bde

1700
13/2/18

88 Bde
29 Div

Confidential.

War Diary

of

1st Bn. The Essex Regiment

for Month of January 1918.

Volume 35.

1 Essex Regt
Vol 26

1st BN. THE ESSEX REGIMENT.
WAR DIARY
INTELLIGENCE SUMMARY.
(Erase heading not required.)

Army Form C. 2118.

Place	Date	Hour	Summary of Events and Information	Remarks and references to Appendices
ROYAN (LEBIEZ)	Nov 1st		Battalion Training	
	" 2nd			
	" 3rd		Battalion left ROYAN at 8am and arrived at CHAMPAGNE-LE-BOULONNAIS at 4pm (Distance about 20 miles). The roads were in a very bad condition owing to the heavy fall of snow.	
	" 4th		The Battalion left CHAMPAGNE-LE-BOULONNAIS at 8.30am arriving at BOISDINGHEM at 5.15 pm (Distance about 15 miles) The roads were still in a very bad condition.	
	" 5th		BOISDINGHEM. The Bn rested today after the Route march.	
	" 6th		Bn attended Church parade held in a Hanger as the Flying Grounds.	
	" 7th		Gunnery on Range 9.30 am to 11.30 pm and "good days work".	
	" 8th		Another fine day. The Bn underwent training under Company arrangements.	
	" 9th		Snowed all day. Lectures	
	" 10th		Battalion training	
	" 11th		Brigade practice for presentation of awards	
	" 12th		The Brigade formed up and the presentation of awards for the Cambrai operation	

WAR DIARY
or
INTELLIGENCE SUMMARY.
(Erase heading not required.)

Army Form C. 2118.

Instructions regarding War Diaries and Intelligence Summaries are contained in F. S. Regs., Part II. and the Staff Manual respectively. Title pages will be prepared in manuscript.

Place	Date	Hour	Summary of Events and Information	Remarks and references to Appendices
	Jan 12th (Contd)		were made by the Divisional Commander	
	Jan 13th		Bn attended Church Parade	
	" 14th		Bn Training	
	" 15th		A Brigade tactical exercise was carried out the day ended by pouring rain	
	" 16th		Bn Training	
	" 17th		The Bn left BOISDINGHEM at 6.30 a.m and entrained at WIZERNES for BRANDHOEK arriving at 3 p.m. We then proceeded to WARRINGTON CAMP (on POPERINGHE — YPRES ROAD) Rain and sleet nearly all day.	
	" 18th		The Bn left BRANDHOEK at 2 p.m. and marched to ST JEAN arriving at 7 p.m. One Company was billeted at CALIFORNIA CAMP and 3 Companies and Bn H.Q. at JUNCTION CAMP	
	" 19th		Company Commanders went to select reserve line to be held by the Battalion in case of emergency.	
	" 20th		Battalion employed drawing trench stores and carrying, ducks boards to front line.	
	" 21st		Battalion drawing trench stores	

Army Form C. 2118.

WAR DIARY
or
INTELLIGENCE SUMMARY
(Erase heading not required.)

Place	Date	Hour	Summary of Events and Information	Remarks and references to Appendices
	Jan 22nd		The Bn. were employed cleaning the streets and preparing a line of defence.	
	" 23rd		Bn. cleaning streets and constructing strong points. The ground here was so very hard that the men experienced difficulty in these days full of water and consequently the work was very difficult.	
	" 24th		Do. Do.	
	" 25th		Working parties to prepare the new sunken wire screen position at BELLEVUE.	
	" 26th		"X" "Y" and "Z" Companies relieved the 1st Bn. LANCASHIRE FUSILEERS at BELLEVUE at 4 p.m. The relief was completed at 7.30 p.m. "W" Company was left behind at CALIFORNIA CAMP for the purpose of supplying parties for digging.	
	" 27th		Coys cleaning strong points at BELLEVUE. "X" "Y" and "Z" Companies living in an outhouse and improving their shelter. The Coys carrying supplies carrying parties to front line with pickets and wire.	
	" 28th		Coys very much the same. Shelters BELLEVUE throughout the day were very much improved drawing attention on BELLEVUE. Coys been d.a carrying parties. The weather was thick, although the enemy shelled on position on + off all day.	

WAR DIARY
or
INTELLIGENCE SUMMARY.
(Erase heading not required.)

Army Form C. 2118.

Place	Date	Hour	Summary of Events and Information	Remarks and references to Appendices
	Jan 29		It was fairly clear the whole day and movements for parties on X	
			off all day. Parties of ROYAL ENGINEERS who were working on the road were the principal fire and were dispersed. Much trouble has been caused by these parties congregating in a dense clump	
	Jan 30		On this day our rifle fire and several aeroplane flew over our lines. Attempts of our aircraft. The shelling to the morning was never slight but	
			were engaged by our aircraft. The shelling to the morning was very slight but	
			at 3.35 pm the enemy put one close 50 feet ahead. Our men were effectual	
	Jan 31		lot of the fire but it was all overhead	
			Bn Establm [?] relieves us side front line. W Company on the right X Company in the centre and Z Company on the left. Y Company were in support of Gurkberg Ridge. We relieved the NEWFOUNDLAND REGT and Suppers & Miners & Cavalier on this way up the whole of the road where 5 & 6 were attempt but a great deal of caution by the enemy artillery and practically no movement was possible except during [?] weather.	
			~~It was very misty all day but the enemy artillery was both Franco-Serb~~	
			~~Enemy machine guns fired every break but the majority of them shots went well overhead~~	

www.ingramcontent.com/pod-product-compliance
Lightning Source LLC
Chambersburg PA
CBHW081540160426
43191CB00011B/1805